BATAVIA PLACES AND THE PEOPLE WHO CALLED THEM HOME

Batavia, Illinois

MARILYN ROBINSON

D1453782

BATAVIA PLACES AND THE PEOPLE WHO CALLED THEM HOME

Copyright © 1996, MARILYN ROBINSON

Printed in the United States of America

Publisher's Cataloging-in-Publication Data

Robinson, Marilyn, 1931-   .
  Batavia places and the people who called them home /Marilyn Robinson.
  Includes index.
  ISBN 0-923889-21-3
  1. Architecture--Illinois--Batavia 2.Batavia (Ill.)--Buildings, structures, etc. 3. Genealogy--Illinois 4. Genealogy--New York. I. Title
                        977.323   95-92614
                                                        CIP

DEDICATION

To the men and women who forged Batavia out of the woods and prairie and all who have ever called it home.

ACKNOWLEDGMENTS

I wish to thank each of the following for their help in writing this book.

All who told me about their homes
and
Dr. Robert Barnes
Neil Benson
Judy Dykman
Jana Fitting
Carla Hill
Arlene Nick
Richard Palmer
Mary Peterson
Nancy Prichard
Daniel Russo
Liz Spalding
Fran Steiner
Ruth Strand
William Wood

TABLE OF CONTENTS

INTRODUCTION

We shape our buildings; thereafter, they shape us.—
Winston Churchill

Buildings change as people do. As men prosper or families grow, add-ons are made. Fashion alters style. Picture windows replace smaller ones. Decks replace porches. As technology develops, plumbing and electrical appliances are added. The computer spawns home offices.

A house and its residents mold to each other. Each building has its own biography. Much of Batavia's charm comes from the many fine buildings that line her streets. Some date from the earliest days of the village and tell their story through their genealogy.

My interest in Batavia history began in the snowy winter of 1978-79 when I moved to the front portion of the beautiful old home at 325 South Batavia Avenue. I learned that it was built in 1858. I researched the history of Batavia and wrote **"Little Town in a Big Woods"** there.

Shortly after that book's publication, I ran into Arlene Nick, Publisher of the **Windmill Herald** who asked what my next book would be about. I was cheered by her confidence that I could do another.

"I want to write about some of the old houses in town, I said. Walking around the block—Union Avenue to Jefferson Street, Elm Street and back to the Avenue— had increased my interest in the homes on those streets.

"Oh, I'm looking for someone to write a series on some of the historic houses," she said. My first article appeared in the **Windmill Herald** on July 11, 1990. Had it not been for our chance meeting three weeks earlier, this book might never have come to be.

The buildings included here do not reflect in any way the only historic ones in Batavia. Most were chronicled in the **Windmill Herald** from 1990-94. There was no plan as to which buildings I researched. Some were done because I knew the owners. Some were chosen because of the significance of an early owner. Others were chosen because Arlene or their current owners asked me to write about them. Most are at least 100 years old. Many bear a Batavia Historical Society plaque. The articles aren't updated in regard to interior features. The descriptions are from original interviews.

As I dug into land records, old newspapers, personal diaries, probate records, and other sources I learned that the more one researches, the cloudier a fact may become. There are contradictions in records and errors in newspaper articles and books. Legends and myths are perpetuated even when official records prove otherwise. There are errors in my earlier writings because I didn't dig deep enough. Those I found were corrected here. I have tried to be as accurate as possible with the resources available.

The purpose of this book is to tell the story of Batavia places and to introduce those connected with them so that they become more than just names on a page. To do that, it is sometimes necessary to repeat what others have written.

Signatures of early citizens were found on old public documents filed at the Depot Museum. Street names and addresses are those in use today. Bold type material was previously published, usually in the **Windmill Herald**.

Enjoy your walk through Batavia in these pages. May you come to know a bit better some who have called Batavia home.

Marilyn Robinson

BATAVIA PLACES AND THE PEOPLE WHO CALLED THEM HOME

Batavia, Illinois

HEAD OF BIG WOODS

On March 14, 1837, Isaac Wilson wrote to Rev. J. M. Peck, a Baptist minister, describing the Fox River Valley.[1]

> "The big woods is the largest body of timber in the state. They lie on the east side, adjoining the Fox River for about ten miles in length and are from two to four miles wide. There are many kinds of trees, and the soil is generally a dark sandy loam, generally a little undulating, but sometimes quite level. The big woods is thickly settled on all sides, and the four-mile prairie between it and the DuPage River is all claimed and considerably settled."[2]

Wilson's concept of "considerably settled" meant that every few miles there was a cabin. He couldn't have imagined what "considerably settled" means in the 1990s.

John vanNortwick first came to the Fox River in February 1837. He wrote to his wife Maria about his fourteen day trip from Penn Yann, New York. Today this trip can be driven by car in one long day. John wrote,

> "After you get ten miles from Chicago, you find a rolling prairie with occasionally a grove of timber. The soil is a black muck and very rich, and I think was by far the finest farming country I have ever saw. [*sic*] I think the farms about the Fox River the best I have seen, there being more and plenty of timber for farming purposes."[3]

The best location for settlers to a new area was in or near a timber which provided wood for protection from the elements, wild animals, and Indians. It was also easier to clear timberland than to cut the tall, tough prairie grass. In 1835 William vanNortwick wrote to his son John, **"It takes four of the best yoke of oxen to plow the tough prairie grass to clear a spot to raise corn or wheat."**[4] Almost no settlers were found on the prairie in this area prior to 1837.

Settlers were in constant fear of prairie fires. A fire, especially in the fall, in the high grass (sometimes 12 to

15 feet high) would sweep over the prairie faster than a horse could run. A settler often burned a strip of ground surrounding his farm to prevent the flames from destroying his crops and buildings. Neighbors would frequently fight a fire long into the night to help save another's buildings.

Settlers arrived at Head of Big Woods and claimed nearly all the timber land before 1836. To establish a claim in 1833, a man simply marked off what he wanted. Later he was required to register his claim in the Federal Land Office in Chicago.

The government had not yet surveyed this new state called Illinois, and difficulties soon arose among those early settlers in relation to the boundaries and priority of the claims of each. There were bitter arguments between neighbors when one accused the other of "jumping my claim." Because men had set their own boundaries in no particular pattern, and in some cases had put improvements upon the land, disputes had to be settled.

Government surveys of Kane County took place in 1839-40, and in 1842 the land was open for sale by the United States Government. Men who had staked claims now had to pay the government $1.25 an acre for it. A man had to get to the land office before someone else purchased what he claimed was his land. If this happened, he would have to buy it from that purchaser who could ask any price he chose. This process of buying open land from the government was called preemption.

James Rockwell described what it was like during this time in November 1841.

> **"The late preemption law has created much excitement here. The Big Woods are full of preemption shanties and some on the prairies. The prairie on which I made some improvement has been entered upon and a log cabin erected. I sold a part of it for enough to pay what it cost me. There was one quarter section on the rear of the school section that was marked around at the expense of Mother**

[vanNortwick] and the girls. It was thought best by Father [vanNortwick] that I should take preemption upon that, and Mother has always been very anxious that it should be secured. I think it more valuable than that further on the prairie. I accordingly erected a shanty and lodged in it one night and left Margaret [Mrs. Rockwell] to occupy it until I went to the office and secured my preemption. My twenty-two acres of timber land lying on two different quarter sections have been preempted by two different individuals. In order to get their own and secure the land from interlopers, a man must take the land belonging to several and after the preemption is taken, deed it back to the rightful owners. The eighty acres that Father bought has been preempted, but I am told the man will release one half of it. I think timber land cannot be bought in the Big Woods after a title is obtained for less than $15 per acre. Father thinks he should be well contented to live on the prairie. He will take eighty acres of what I preempted and make some improvement on it this winter and build a house in the spring."[5]

Prior to the land coming on the market in 1842, many roads had been located by common consent as claim lines were established. Many of these remain nearly as originally located, and some of the old claim lines still govern land boundaries.

The first land transaction in Kane County was recorded on January 21, 1837. It was an agreement for a deed between James Crow and Wallace Hotchkiss for 300 acres of prairie and 160 acres of timber on the east side of the Fox River in Batavia which Crow had claimed.[6]

---

[1] J. M. Peck published a monthly called **The Western Baptist** at Rockspring, Illinois. He also wrote **A GAZETTEER OF ILLINOIS** published in 1837 in which he gives a similar description of Big Woods. It's possible that Wilson's letter was written in reply to a request from Peck for a description of the Fox River Valley for his book.

[2] Published in the **Peoria Register and North-Western Gazetteer,**

dated Head of Big Woods, Kane County, Illinois, March 14, 1837.
[3] William B. vanNortwick, **vanNORTWICK GENEALOGY** (1971) 89.
[4] vanNortwick 62.
[5] vanNortwick 194-95.
[6] **Book 1**, Recorder's Office, Geneva.

[A page of handwritten signatures including: James Risk, S. Booth, M. W. Lord, G. W. Makepeace, L. P. Barker, Geo. B. Moss, Christopher Payne (his mark), N. S. Young, Elizabeth Payne (her mark), Jacob Grimes, C. W. Shumway, Geo Bassett, Thompson Mead, Alfred Churchill, Arthur Vanderson, and others.]

EARLY LAND DEVELOPERS

William hile men were founding a new settlement at Head of Big Woods and were bringing their families to the Fox River Valley, Andrew Jackson was President of the United States. A new Democratic and the Whig party were forming.

The Black Hawk War was finally over. President Jackson had ordered the Indians moved west of the Mississippi River.

A twenty-five-year-old backwoodsman named Abraham Lincoln was entering politics as an assemblyman in Springfield.

By the time Isaac Wilson arrived, Martin VanBuren was America's eighth president.

How much this political environment influenced early settlers to come to this settlement can only be guessed. No doubt the possibility of making money was what enticed some to this valley, rich with natural resources.

TITUS HOWE

Titus Howe arrived in 1834. A carpenter by trade, he failed in his attempt at industry in Big Woods, according to most accounts, including references in the vanNortwick letters.

Titus knew that whoever had the rights to the waterpower could be successful. He made a verbal agreement to buy some land from Joel McKee in order to build a dam at the north end of the island. William vanNortwick owned the land on the east side of the river, and William and Titus negotiated to share in the building of a dam and the waterpower it would produce.

When Isaac Wilson arrived in Head of Big Woods, he tried to join in the deal through Titus, whom he had known in New York. While William was absent, Isaac drew up a contract that would permit the vanNortwicks only a one-third share in the dam and its waterpower instead of the one-half share Howe and vanNortwick had negotiated. William refused the new deal and cut Howe out of their original one.

McKee grew tired of waiting for Titus to raise the money to buy his land, so he sold it to vanNortwick instead. Father and son now owned land on both sides of the river, so they hurriedly began a dam to beat Titus. William would oversee the job, and John would pay for it.

After his deal with vanNortwick fell through, Titus moved to the south end of the island and built a dam and a frame for a saw mill. Unfortunately, a flood the following spring washed away the dam and part of the saw mill. Because he lacked funds to repair the damage, he sold what was left to the vanNortwicks who had been biding their time, waiting for Titus to run out of money. Now they had nearly total control of waterpower in Head of Big Woods.

After his financial set back, Titus went to Yorkville. In 1842 his land belonged to George Makepeace. George sold it to Harvey Bristol who later sold it to Elijah S. Town.

Fifty-seven years after leaving Big Woods, a son of Howe's, C. S. of Huron, Ohio, recalled the story of the dam building a bit differently. He told the **Batavia Herald.**

> "I came with my father in 1834 when the Indians roamed the prairie and there were no homes. One "squatter" had a claim staked out and was catching his living out of the raging Fox and shooting coyotes.
>
> "Father purchased the squatter's claim, and the squatter moved on. At the time there was only one family, Isaac Wilson's and one lone gentleman, McKee."[1]

With the help of his sons, Howe, Sr., hewed out blocks from the timber and erected a home. After that he built the first dam across the river and laid the foundation of industries by erecting a saw mill. After getting everything in good running order, he sold out to a good advantage and went to Yorkville. There he built the first dam across the river and a grist mill according to C. S.[2]

Titus did build the Yorkville saw mill in 1837.[3]

It's believed that the north section of the Greek Revival house at 211 Main Street contains part of Howe's original Batavia cabin.

The Eastern Conglomerate

A conglomerate of eastern capitalists, Joseph Churchill, George Makepeace, Lester Barker, John vanNortwick and Alanson House, purchased much of the land that later formed the original village of Batavia. The men called their firm, formed in July 1839, vanNortwick, Barker, House & Co. Isaac Wilson and Joel McKee tried to become associated with the men, but when they weren't embraced, they competed against them for land and water power.

Other men were involved with the company, including Charles Ballard, who was married to John's sister Fanny, and James Rockwell who was married to Margaret, another of John's sisters. The marriages made these men brothers-in-law in addition to business associates. It was common for brothers-in-law to be in business together. It kept the money in the family.

Others in the conglomerate were related. Alanson House was a brother-in-law to George R. Makepeace and Lester Barker, for these men were married to House's sisters, Rhoda Makepeace and Sybil Barker.

Joseph Churchill came to Batavia in 1838 as the village's first attorney. He served as an Illinois state senator in 1838-39 with Abraham Lincoln.

Although he was successful in real estate and law here, he moved to Iowa in 1854 and lived there the rest of his life. Joseph was a son-in-law of Judge Isaac Wilson. When Wilson was named Batavia's first postmaster in 1841, the post office was located in Joseph's law office.[4] His clerk was in charge of the mail.[5] It was in 1841 that Wilson changed the village's name to Batavia.

In the 1850 census, Joseph was the second richest man in Batavia with $10,000 worth of real estate. Only John vanNortwick was richer with land valued at $18,000.

George Makepeace made a number of trips back and forth from New York. Eventually he settled in Batavia, but he was accused by William vanNortwick of using company supplies and labor to build his home. William told John that Makepeace owed the company $65 because of what he'd appropriated from the mill.[6] Eventually George exchanged his in-town property for a farm and moved away from the village.[7]

Lester Barker, also, made many trips west to see to his investments and to report to House and vanNortwick in New York.

John vanNortwick made only one visit to Batavia before he came to stay. He visited in 1835 and returned to settle in 1846 when he began work on the Galena and Chicago Railroad. Until he moved to Batavia, he relied on his father and his father-in-law, Meredith Mallory, to run his affairs for him on the Fox River.

Alanson House lived in Utica, New York. He never married and made a number of trips to Batavia from New York. Back in New York, he would meet with vanNortwick and the others on river boats, in saloons, or hotels to make his reports.

He speculated in real estate in Batavia where he died in November 1849. In January before his death, he came here to live in order to get a handle on his investments which were going bad. He had tried for a couple of years to get vanNortwick to buy him out. **"This speculation of ours has just about ruined me,"** he wrote John in 1841.[8]

He wrote again later,

> "The Fox River speculation has been a sour affair
> for me. I have been bled more fully in this matter
> than anyone else. I hope I shall be able to weather
> the tempest. I want you to buy my interest at a
> bargain. Make me an offer. We need to meet. The
> property is good and can be productive if managed
> with any kind of skill."[9]

William vanNortwick was the first of the eastern conglomerate to settle in Big Woods. He arrived in 1835, and using son John's money, began industrial development, including the building of a dam and a saw and flouring mill. House and Barker were investors in these first ventures. Eventually House owned the mill and after his death, Joel McKee and George B. Moss purchased them.

The wheeling and dealing of these men is described in letters between John, William, and Alanson.[10] While there is no actual admission of guilt nor evidence of illegal maneuvers, there was borrowing from men who were known to owe Titus Howe money, delayed payments of those loans so that the lenders couldn't pay Howe, the trading of land, and the working off of debts that made it impossible for Howe's debtors to pay him. Howe eventually ran out of cash.

James Rockwell wasn't a partner in the eastern conglomerate, but he was an integral part of what went on in early Batavia. He was a native of Connecticut, born during the War of 1812.

Rockwell had learned the cabinetmaker's trade in Connecticut, but he hoped to do better in the West. He traveled as far as Detroit by water and walked the rest of the way to Chicago. It took him eight days.

In Chicago he built a furniture-making factory where he employed twelve men. When state banks failed, he closed his business and moved to Batavia in February 1838. Soon after, he met Margaret vanNortwick and they were married.

9

James helped his father-in-law while he also manufactured furniture and ran a general store. He was a religious man and may have frowned on some of the business dealings of his friends and relatives. He assisted in the organization of the First Methodist Church in Chicago and in Batavia.[11]

The conglomerate's biggest financial troubles began after the government opened the land for sale. By 1844 all of the partners had sold out or traded their joint holdings to John.

The first platting of the village of Batavia is attributed to John vanNortwick in 1844. The plat is recorded as Barker, House & Co.'s. It's in the area of the vanNortwick dam and extends from the river to VanBuren Street and a little north of Fayette Street, south to State Street.

There were several men who were prominent as land developers beside those associated with the Eastern Conglomerate.[12]

Elijah Shumway Town

Growing up in Granville, New York, Elijah felt a calling to serve God. At twenty-three, he served at the Indian Mission at Mayhew, Mississippi, ministering to the natives. He stayed there for six years during which time he met and married Hannah Cone.

In 1833 he took Hannah home to meet his folks, Ben and Mary Town. He'd heard about the great northwest and its opportunities, so he talked Hannah into taking the long riverboat trip to Fort Dearborn, Illinois. There they got a wagon and crossed to the head of Big Woods, spending their first nights with the Christopher Paynes who had the only cabin in Big Woods at the time. Though there were a few others at the settlement, they hadn't raised cabins yet. Elijah built his about a half-mile south of Wilson Street on Batavia Avenue.

During his years in Batavia, Elijah became a land-owner and a successful contractor. A newspaper wrote of his mills which were located on the west side of the Island at about First Street.

> **"Everything about E. S. Town and Company's Flour-ing and Saw Mill, lumber yard, etc., denotes sub-stantial prosperity, and the constant whir of the saw and grinding of the mill stones evidences a large business."**[13]

Town's partner was Sackett Booth in this business. They had started Island Mills seven years earlier.

Most famous of Elijah's construction jobs is the stone-work on the foundation of the Congregational Church on Batavia Avenue which he did in 1855. He also built the limestone house later known as Lockwood Hall and the limestone house on South Batavia Avenue called Stone Manor.

He encouraged the education of Batavia's youth by helping four other men build Batavia Institute at the top of Union Avenue.

In addition to his land holdings and construction work, Elijah owned a limestone quarry for ten years. Many of the stone buildings in town were built of his stone. He also ran the Batavia Barrel Manufacturing Company on River and State Streets.

Dr. Denison K. Town

Dr. Town, an M.D., arrived in Batavia about 1839 or 40. He was a younger brother of Elijah S. and had attended medical lectures in New Haven, Connecticut. As a phy-sician, D. K. treated such ailments in Batavia as bilious fever, dysentery, whooping cough, and ague (a malarial fever) which was quite prevalent and was caused by drinking impure and stagnant water in streets, pools, and sloughs. Town practiced medicine in Batavia until 1862 when he quit to concentrate on real estate.

In 1850 the Kane County tax list shows that D. K. had $7,000 worth of real estate. In addition to these holdings, he also owned a railroad car factory on the north side of First Street at the river in 1857.

In 1867 Town lived on the east side of Batavia Avenue, south of Union Avenue. He built a large home on the west side of Batavia Avenue that was torn down in 1962 to make way for Lincoln Court. It was a massive, strong house that resisted the wrecking ball. When the demolition team swung the ball at the house, it did not give way; but the ball broke. The spectators applauded.

In December 1856 Town bought the entire block bounded by Batavia Avenue, Jefferson and Elm Streets, and Union Avenue from his brother Elijah. He is credited with planting the beautiful maple trees that line Union Avenue and Elm Street today.

Two subdivisions on the east side bear his name. D. K. Town's Addition extends between Prairie and College Streets from approximately Elizabeth to Madison Streets. His second addition is approximately between the old C. B. & Q. Railroad tracks and Prairie Street, from Adams to Pine Street.

Israel Shipman Pelton Lord, M.D.
Monroe Nathan Lord

Dr. Israel S. P. Lord[14] was a practicing physician who came to Batavia some time before June 1836. This makes him the first physician in Big Woods although many sources say it was D. K. Town. Israel was still practicing in 1848 when his father-in-law, Isaac Wilson, died for he was Wilson's physician.

Israel married Isaac's daughter Mary in New York in 1831. They had six children; all but the first were born in Batavia between 1836-52.

Israel went to California in 1849 to try his luck in the gold fields. He left Mary here to tend to their $3,000 worth of real estate. He came back to a lonesome Mary two years later.

Israel and his brother, Monroe Nathan, owned a great deal of land on the east side. Monroe once owned most of the land in the first block of East Wilson Street, starting at the river.

Israel lived on the southwest corner of Washington Avenue and Wilson Street, and Monroe and his family lived on the northwest corner of VanBuren and State Streets.

After his return from California, Israel stayed in Batavia for ten years until he moved to Chicago for a time before returning to New York. He eventually moved again to Los Angeles, where he died in 1896.

Mary Wilson Lord died in New York in 1874. She had requested that she be buried in Batavia, and her wishes were honored. In 1894 Israel asked that Mary be exhumed and sent to California for burial.

Her remains were unearthed by East Side Cemetery Sexton S. J. Hampton. The coffin had a glass lid so Hampton could see the corpse. It looked just as it had when it was buried twenty years before.[15]

Dr. Lord became nationally known as a physician. He left many notes and journals, some of which are in the Huntington Museum in California.

Monroe was an insurance agent for at least some of the time he was in Batavia. He was born in New York City and died in Benton Harbor, Michigan. His wife was Jane Austin of New York.

Captain Christian B. Dodson

C. B. Dodson's first land development might not have been considered in Head of Big Woods, but it is within Batavia today. In June 1834 he settled a mile and one-half south of the village, at the mouth of Mill Creek. He immediately began building the first saw mill in Kane County along with a store for trading with the Indians.

That same year he formed a partnership with Archibald Clybourne of Chicago, and they began a settlement which they called Clybournville.

The men hoped to develop a large trade with the Indians. Their trading post was often filled with skins which were purchased and sold for almost nothing. They hired a young Indian boy to stay in the store to converse with the Indians and to teach Dodson and Clybourne the language of the Pottawatomies.

In 1835 Dodson and Clybourne took a contract from the United States Government to remove the local Indians to Council Bluffs, Iowa.

After he returned from this trip, C. B. settled in Geneva; and John Peter Schneider, a founder of North Aurora, took over the operation of his mill. Dodson served in the Civil War with a company organized in Geneva. He died in 1891 in Geneva and is buried there with his wife, Harriett Warren, a daughter of the founder of Warrenville.

---

[1] This would not have been correct.

[2] **Batavia Herald**, November 26, 1893.

[3] A **BICENTENNIAL HISTORY OF KENDALL COUNTY, ILLINOIS** (The Kendall County Bicentennial Commission, 1976) 104.

[4] Where this was is not known. Churchill owned a great deal of land on the east side of the river adjoining his father-in-law's. He also owned some land on the west side.

[5] vanNortwick 179.

[6] vanNortwick 206.

[7] Makepeace owned several pieces of land to the north of the village later on, so it may have been one of those pieces that he got from vanNortwick.

[8] vanNortwick 198.

[9] vanNortwick 204.

[10] vanNortwick 205.

[11] **BIOGRAPHICAL RECORD OF KANE COUNTY** (Chicago: The S. J. Clarke Publishing Co. 1898) 344.

[12] Many other men came to Batavia and preempted land. The settlement of the village was not limited to those mentioned here. The ones included came early and dealt in the buying and selling of land. Others came, bought pieces of land, settled and raised their families.

[13] **Aurora Beacon**, May 10, 1866.

[14] Thanks to Dr. Robert Barnes of Batavia for sharing his material

on the Lord brothers and for his permission to use it here.
[15] This story was originally reported in the **Batavia Herald**, January, 1894.

Photo courtesy of the Batavia Historical Society

cabin similar to those of the earliest settlers

BATAVIA PLACES

remains of C. B. Dodson's mill

vanNortwick dam at the north end of the riverwalk

CHRISTOPHER PAYNE

The first homes on the land that was to become Batavia were the temporary wigwams made of buffalo hides and the long houses built of logs and sod belonging to the Pottawatomie Indians who resided here.

There were log cabins as early as 1835 on the east side of the river at about Fayette Street. They belonged to William Vandeventer and William vanNortwick. On the west side just north of North Avenue was the cabin and store of Joel McKee.

The first settler's home in Kane County was in Head of Big Woods. It was built by Christopher Payne[1] in 1833 about a quarter of a mile northwest of the intersection of Kirk Road and Wilson Street. A boulder with a plaque, placed there by the Batavia Historical Society, tells the location.

In 1933 a group of Batavia men excavated the spot where it was thought the Payne cabin stood along Mahoney's Creek. They found bits of glass window pane and the pit and back brick wall of a fireplace. Because it was unusual for a pioneer cabin, particularly an isolated one, to have glass windows and a brick fireplace, it is not conclusive that these were installed by Payne. He may have brought the glass and brick from Naperville as it was only a day's ride away, but it may also be that a later owner upgraded the cabin.

By tracing the outline of the cabin, the diggers found the door had been on the south side as was usual to keep out the cold north wind. The cabin measured 14 by 16 feet, smaller than some rooms in homes today. There was a kind of cellar 7 x 7 feet which contained a fresh water spring. This may have been built as a hiding place from Indians. Enough pieces of wood were found to substantiate that it was a log cabin.[2]

An early settler like Payne brought little besides his ax and rifle. His first labor was to fell trees and build a log cabin. It was usually from 14 to 16 feet square and was frequently built without glass, nails, hinges, or locks.

> "To erect a cabin, the builder first laid large logs in position as sills for a foundation. On these he placed strong sleepers, and on the sleepers he laid rough-hewed puncheons to serve as floors. Logs were then built up to the desired height for the eaves. On the ends of the building, he placed poles, which were longer than the other end-logs, which projected some eighteen or so inches over the sides. On the projecting ends, he placed the butting-pole which served to give the line to the first row of clap-boards. These were split, and as the gables of the cabin were built up, were laid in such a manner that they lapped a third of their length. They were often kept in place by the weight of a heavy pole, laid across the roof parallel to the ridge pole.

> "The house was then chinked and daubed with a coarse mortar. At one end of the house the builder made the fireplace for cooking and heating. He sometimes covered the ceiling with the pelts of the raccoon, opossum, and wolf to add warmth to his dwelling. Sheets of strong paper, well saturated with coon grease or bear oil, were carefully tacked over an opening in a side of the cabin to provide light."[3]

It is not known exactly how much land Payne claimed. It appears to have extended west to Prairie Street, east a fifth mile past Kirk Road, south to a little beyond Cleveland Street and north, a little beyond Elizabeth Street.

In 1835 Payne sold his claim, including the cabin, to Isaac Wilson for $1,500. This was a great sum of money at the time and shows the extent of Wilson's resources and the apparent size of the claim.

Payne was born in Pennsylvania ten years after the American Revolution began in 1786. When he was fourteen, his family moved to Ohio. He fought in the War of 1812 as an Indian scout in Indiana.

Traveling by oxen cart with his wife Elizabeth and their nearly adult children, they arrived at Big Woods in

1833. They opened their cabin to families that followed soon after. It's apparent that Christopher didn't really like civilization for he soon moved on, finally staying in Wisconsin where he and Elizabeth died.[4] They are buried near Portage, Wisconsin.

In 1878 Elisha Town said of Payne, **"He was one of the roughest men in the world, but possessed of a generous and kind nature."**[5]
C. B. Dodson agreed with Town.

> **"Payne was one of nature's noblemen. He was extremely hospitable and his little sixteen foot, square log shanty was frequently crowded with strangers. It has long been torn down and forgotten. It may also be considered the first tavern in Batavia as Payne entertained all the explorers who sought his door."**[6]

---

[1] Many previous local history books say that Payne's middle name was Columbus. Dr. Robert Barnes who is doing an in-depth study of the Payne family finds no evidence in official records that Payne ever had a middle name. Thanks to Dr. Barnes for allowing the use of some of his research in this chapter.

[2] Originally published July 11, 1990.

[3] **HISTORY OF MADISON COUNTY, ILLINOIS** (Edwardsville, Illinois: W. R. Brink & Co. 1882) 93, 94.

[4] He in 1871; she in 1869.

[5] **KANE COUNTY, PAST AND PRESENT** (Chicago: Wm. LeBaron, Jr. & Co. 1878) 299.

[6] **KANE COUNTY, PAST AND PRESENT** 299.

The spot where Christopher Payne built his cabin. The forked tree is in the middle of where his cabin would have been. It's possible to feel, but not see, a ridge running from the second tree at the left of the forked tree to the first large one to the right of it, a space of 14 feet.

The ridge is about three feet in front of the row of trees. It's apparently the remainder of the excavation which was done in 1933. The spot is about 430 feet north of Wilson Street, just to the west of Mahoney Creek, and 70 feet west of the light poles that run along the west side of Batavia Apartments. (Photo taken in November 1994.)

JUDGE ISAAC WILSON
406 East Wilson Street

Isaac Wilson arrived in Head of Big Woods in 1835. He bought Christopher Payne's claim, making him the owner of most of the land from Kirk Road to Prairie Street along Wilson Street. The dirt path that crossed his land became known as Wilson Street.

Isaac was born in Vermont in 1780, just four years after the Declaration of Independence, but spent much of his young adult life in New York.

He served as a Cavalry Captain in the War of 1812 and after that was in the New York State Assembly for a year. Then for three years he was a State Senator.

He served as Judge of the County Court for a couple of years, and later was a member of the 18th Congress for ten months until his election opponent, Parmenio Adams, contested his victory. He won, so Isaac returned to service as a county judge until coming here.

Isaac was one of the founders of the East Side Cemetery, serving as the first president of that board. Batavia was only eleven years old when some of its citizens met in George Fowler's general store to establish the cemetery. They bought two acres of land for $80 from George which was the start of a home for deceased citizens of Batavia.

Isaac married Susannah Doran January 5, 1800. The couple had six children. Isaac brought Susannah here to a primitive home on the prairie. Their children were all grown by then, so the Payne's log cabin was really enough until he built the then spacious home on Wilson and Prairie Streets.

Daughters Susan and Delia married Churchill brothers. Fanny married James Risk who had come to Big Woods very early, too, with his brother-in-law, Joel McKee. Mary married Israel Lord.

21

Emma married Arthur Vanderveer. Eliza and her husband Mr. Ewell stayed in New York. Isaac, Jr., was a judge in Kane County.

The oldest remaining residence in Batavia was built by Isaac Wilson about 1843. It was worth $800 in 1850. Susannah lived in the house until she died in 1848.

The home is currently owned by Peter and Becky McIntyre. In 1977 they purchased it from William Petit, who had owned it as a rental property for eighteen years.

Others who have lived in the house include Michael Monahan in the 1910s, Chauncey Hambel in the 1920s, and James Kearns in the 1930-50s.

The front door with the stairway and hall right inside the door are reminiscent of early Greek revival architecture. The one and one-half story house is like those still found in upstate New York. This makes McIntyre wonder if the judge duplicated his eastern home here on the Illinois prairie.

The original house had a front living room, a large kitchen, and a small dining room separated from the kitchen by a wall with a wide arched doorway. The wall is gone.

The rear wing of the house served as a wood shed and contains a fieldstone-lined cistern. Between the kitchen and the rear wing are two rooms that were probably bedrooms. When the McIntyres pulled the inside pine siding from the walls in these rooms, they found plaster and small scraps of wallpaper that appeared to be of a bedroom design. One of the rooms is quite small so may have been a maid's room. Today the two rooms are the kitchen and bathroom.

Upstairs are three bedrooms with large closets containing windows. A patch of plaster has been removed to expose the hand-hewn laths.

When the McIntyres first purchased the home, they had to camp out in it for six months before they began slowly to renovate it. They did the plumbing first, then the wiring and the furnace. They began at the front and took off the asbestos and wood siding to insulate the house. They slowly redid the outside, using as much of the original wood siding as they could save.

They found the roof sheeting boards, the posts, and the beams were of walnut; all remain. The hand-hewn beams in the basement are round.

The staircase is walnut, but the railing and most of the balusters are gone. Those remaining are about one inch square. Marks on the first step show that the missing newel post was about four inches square.

Hidden inside a wall of the kitchen was the original brick fireplace containing the woodwork, oven, and cooking crane. These dominate today's living room.

All the floors still have the original boards. The hallway walls were stripped and show that they were originally painted a dark red, much like red-wood today.

All of the original interior doors remain, some with the original Norfolk latches still working. A few upstairs windows contain original glass. Hardware marks on the outside show that there were once shutters on the home.

An 1860 map shows the barn and outhouse stood southeast of the house. An 1871 map shows the house stood on four acres of land with one acre of trees to the south. An 1885 map shows a large one and one-half story stable to the southwest of the home.

The yard is still full of plants indigenous to the prairie. Columbine, ferns, hasta lilies, lily of the valley, and hydrangeas decorate the front of the house. In the backyard, Mrs. McIntyre has added a yellow pioneer rose. The flower is so named because women took cuttings of it as they moved west. McIntyre's great, great grandmother brought the first clipping from New York to southwestern

Michigan. Women of each generation took starts to their new homes, and McIntyre brought a piece of the rose from her mother's Michigan garden to Batavia.

The house was placed on the National Register of Historic Places in 1985.[1]

Isaac died, October 25, 1848, leaving a great deal of land on the east side of Batavia. There are three subdivisions that carry his name.

---

[1] Originally published July 18, 1990.

Photo courtesy of the Batavia Historical Society

oldest remaining residence in Batavia, built by Isaac Wilson about 1843

JACOB GRIMES
215 East Wilson Street

Jacob Grimes was born in New York in 1819, just one year after Illinois became a state. He settled in Batavia in 1845. The 1850 census lists his occupation as a blacksmith. He and his wife Lucy Hoyt have three children listed in the census—May, age 8; Loomis, 6; and William, 2. Jacob's mother Polly lived with the family at the time. Lucy died in 1878.

By 1857 Jacob had changed his profession from blacksmith to dentist and was a partner in Grimes & Wilson—Drugs and Groceries at the corner of River and Wilson Streets. He practiced his dentistry in the store.

At the opening of the Civil War, Jacob raised a company for the 52nd Regiment of the Illinois Volunteers and was elected captain of the group. His sons, William and Loomis, also served in the war.

In 1871 Jacob was stricken with a paralysis and became an invalid. At the time of his death in 1894, he was one of the oldest members of the Baptist Church.

The first recorded sale of the land on which the west part of the Grimes' house sits was in January 1846 when Alanson House sold it to Abner Martin for $50. One year later Martin sold the south half of the land to Polly Grimes for $350 suggesting that he may have built the original west portion of the house. In June 1849 Martin sold the north half of the land to Jacob for $125. In 1847 House sold Polly the land where part of the east portion of the house sits. In 1849 Polly sold all her land to Jacob.

Jacob may have built the house after he acquired the land in 1849; but in the 1850 census, his real estate is valued at what he paid for the land. It seems unlikely that he had added a house to the property.

There is evidence that the two sides of the house were not built at the same time. Neither the brick

nor the interior or exterior walls of the two parts are joined; they abut, so Jacob probably built the east half.

The second story was added in 1886 by Willis Grimes, who purchased the home from his uncle Jacob. Willis' daughter Madge, who was born in the house in 1884, acquired the home and lived in it with her husband William Spencer. Thus it remained in the Grimes family for several generations until Candace Thomas purchased it in 1975.

The ground floor on the west contains a small back room and a larger front room. There is a step down to the two rooms in the east section.

An unusual feature in the three upstairs rooms is the double doors leading to common closets. Each closet can be entered from two rooms.

There is a very low cellar under one-third of the house. The rest has been dug deeper to make room for a furnace. The original outside cellar stair has been covered to make an addition to the house. The cellar walls are of white limestone from Batavia quarries. The cross beams are walnut and still retain some of their bark.

Many years ago there was a white picket fence in front of the home which had to be removed when the Wilson Street hill was cut down, setting the house higher on the hill. The sidewalks surrounding the house were once a mixture of tar and sand.

Thomas said of her home, "There are lots of windows. It's warm and comfortable. I even had fun with the interior doors when I fixed the house. Over the years, the doors had been cut to fit the sagging floors. The steel beams I used to straighten the floors also straightened the woodwork around the doors, and they no longer fit. I moved each one around until I found it a place. I had only one opening left over," she said.[1]

There is a recorded legend that says this house was built by Isaac Wilson. This can't be true. Careful study of land records show that while Isaac did own land to the east, west, and north, he never owned this particular piece. The land and the home were in the Grimes family from 1847-1975.

---

[1]Published July 25, 1990.

Photo courtesy of Batavia Historical Society

Jacob Grimes residence
may be the second oldest remaining home in Batavia

CORNELIUS B. CONDE
HANNAH Q. CONDE
210 North Washington Avenue

Little is recorded in history books about the women who helped their men settle Batavia. Life on the prairie was hard for them. Hannah Quant Conde, the wife of Cornelius B. Conde, was an early settler in Batavia. Their farm was just south of the East Side Cemetery. They built a house on Washington Avenue where some of their descendants still live.

Hannah and C. B. were married in 1836 in New York. The next year they settled in DuPage County where he built wagons.

Five years later, they came to Batavia, and C. B. set up the first blacksmith shop in the village at North River Street. When they arrived here with two babies, it was pretty much a wilderness.

C. B. formed a partnership with John Gregg who is credited with being the first blacksmith in Big Woods. Gregg's shop consisted of only an anvil on a stump.[1] C. B. was also hired by the eastern conglomerate to help collect money that was owed to it.

Hannah kept having babies until by the time of the 1849 Gold Rush in California, they had seven children. That didn't keep C. B. at home; he took an oxen cart and drove it to California staying there for two years searching for gold with some success.

It was hard for Hannah to care for all those children while C. B. was off trying to make a fortune. She didn't do too badly for the children were successful. The oldest, Cornelius, ran a candy store on the island. Frank went into business with his brother-in-law, Mr. Cole on Wilson Street. They made gloves, mittens, and robes from fur pelts. When gloves began to be made of cloth, the brothers-in-law went out of business.

28

A granddaughter became very well known. A Batavia elementary school is named after Louise Conde White. Hannah's daughter Elizabeth was Louise's mother.

After they had been here for a while, C. B. got very homesick. He longed for a visit to Schenectady. They had to travel by boat through the lakes and canals. On the way back after getting off the Erie Canal, they were ready to board the lake boat, but Hannah's hat box was missing. C. B. told her to get on the boat, and he would go back and look for the box. Hannah refused but sat on their trunk on the wharf to wait for him. The lake boat left without them, and they had to wait several days for the next one. Later it was learned that the boat they missed had sunk.

After C. B. returned from California, the family had a pretty good life. He reopened his carriage shop on River Street. Horses would stand quietly with one of their hind hooves between C. B.'s knees as he fitted a new shoe to the hoof. Men liked to gather in the shop to gossip about politics or their farm crops.

C. B. was interested in civic matters, too. He served as a school commissioner, a supervisor, and a town trustee for several years. He served as administrator for people's wills and occasionally acted as guardian to minor children.

C. B. bought property until he had land in several communities. Then all of a sudden in 1885, he died.

When Hannah's youngest, Edwin, became ill with consumption she took care of him during his long illness. He'd never married and lived at home.

Hannah died of a broken heart only a week after Edwin was buried in 1900. She was eighty-three years old.

An unique feature of the Conde house is that it has been owned by the same family since it was built. In June 1846 C. B. bought two lots at the corner of Washington Avenue and Spring Street from Alanson

House, and in 1848 he bought a third lot from House.

It was on one of the first two lots that C. B. built the family home in which his great, great grandson Neal and his family live in 1995. Originally the house, built on a slight hill, had a view overlooking the Fox River.

Hannah's 1900 obituary indicates the house was built in 1849.

By 1900 Peter F. Conde, son of Cornelius and Hannah, and Peter's wife Emaline occupied the home, renting out the south section. In 1904 Frank's son Guy H. and his wife Alma occupied the home and raised their family of five sons there.

In 1960 Neal J. Conde, Jr., the grandson of Guy and Alma and his wife Mary moved into the south section in order to care for Neal's aging grandparents. In 1974 they purchased the house. Their three children, Dawn, Paula, and Neal J., III, make the sixth generation of Condes to live in the homestead.

According to Neal Conde, the original house was the center section with the two wings added one at a time before 1900. An 1869 map shows both wings with two additional wings to the east of the south one. An 1892 map shows the center section and the north wing, but the south wing and its additions are gone. A window exists where plaster was removed from the wall between the center and south sections indicating that the south wing was added to an exterior wall.

The south wing has served as a separate living unit which from time to time was rented to people other than members of the Conde family. Neal and Mary made interior changes as they returned the two-apartment house to a single living unit. They made a summer kitchen into an utility room and the south porch into an office.

There were thirteen rooms originally in the home, but now there are eleven as the south parlor and living room have been joined into one large room. There were once five bedrooms in the house, but one of them is now a sitting room, and one was made into a bathroom. To make a downstairs bathroom, a window and a wall were removed. The side of the house had to be removed to install a shower and tub which were too large to bring through a door. Originally the home had no closets, but some have been built.

The direction of the front stairway has been altered. There is a second stairway in the north wing. Plumbing, electricity, and woodwork have been replaced. The windows have all been repaired with new glass and new frames. The bay window in the south wing has the only original frames. In his remodeling, Conde used a lot of the original oak studs and beams to make trim for the upstairs. He made a plant stand from one of the studs that still has bark on it. He used the original interior doors on the bedroom and closet doors, placing them wherever they fit.

"There are thirty-four windows in the house," said Mary Conde. "I know because I'm the one who painted all of them." There were once three front doors. One led off the first-floor porch into each of the twin parlors in the south and north wings and the third still leads into the center section. This porch and its twin on the second floor remain.

A turn-of-the-century picture shows an iron fence along Washington Avenue and two large chimneys. The fence was sold in the 1940s for scrap iron to aid the war effort. The picture shows beautiful brackets under the roof which are gone as are the decorative posts and shutters. A widow's walk tops the center section. The railing was removed when the roof was replaced.

In the yard are raspberry bushes and rhubarb nearly as old as the house. A hollow maple tree remains in the front yard, but an ancient walnut tree was taken by lightning in 1990. It was from this tree that a Conde boy was nearly hanged by his fun-loving brothers generations ago. Luckily, his grandmother looked out the window in time to cut him down.[2]

---

[1] The **Batavia Congregational Church**, Batavia, Illinois (Batavia, 1935) 7.

[2] Originally published July 17, 1991.

Photo courtesy of the Windmill Herald

Cornelius B. and Hanna Q. Conde residence
still owned by their descendants

Cornelius B Conde

Hannah Conde

JOHN vanNORTWICK
1117 West Main Street

The first pioneers in the West were, as a rule, men who were seeking homes and free lands on which to settle and farm. Later came the hunters and trappers and those who traded with the Indians. Then came the merchants and the men who were to build cities and the superstructures of civilization. Such men were the vanNortwicks who were to construct the great railroads, develop the new country's commercial resources and industrialize Batavia.

William vanNortwick came first in 1835. He left New York via boat down the Ohio River to St. Louis and then up the Illinois River and finally to Big Woods. Most of the early eastern immigrants came by water.

William's letters to his son John indicate that he was in Peoria in April of 1835 and at the Fox River in June.[1]

When William found the Fox River, he saw the potential for waterpower for running factories. There was also the woods which could provide a wealth of lumber.

John was born in 1809, the same year as Abraham Lincoln. He grew up around men whose work it was to make money. His father continually wrote to him of the advantages of investing in this new territory, but he also encouraged him to stay in New York where he worked as a civil engineer and had some job security.

In 1837 when he came to visit his parents, John invested $3,000 in railroads and in efforts to harness water power. He financed the building of a flour and saw mill. The saw mill meant that log cabins were no longer needed, for frame houses could now be built. A large portion of the flour made at the mill went to Chicago, so local farmers gained a profit from raising grain.

John returned to New York to finish his work on the canals. During this time the eastern conglomerate men were active in the fledgling village. Affairs were in disarray out here on the prairie; so when John's work was done in New York, he brought his wife Patty and their five children, William, Eliza, Mary, John, and Lena, to Illinois. It was with his move to Batavia that the vanNortwick industrial empire really grew.

John first accepted a position as the chief developing engineer for the Galena and Chicago Union Railroad. He became consulting engineer for the Chicago, Burlington and Quincy Railroad which was being built from Turner Junction to Aurora. Later he served as president of the C. B. & Q. for eight years.

It was during this time that John became acquainted with Daniel Halladay through John Burnham. John urged Halladay and Burnham to move to Batavia to be closer to the wind mill market. The United States Wind Engine and Pump Co. was established in Batavia in 1857 where Halladay would make his mills.

In 1867 John bought controlling interest in the Batavia Paper Company and became its sole owner two years later. The company expanded into one of the largest paper manufacturing companies in the country. John furnished the farmers with rye seed to get them to raise straw for use in his paper making. At harvest time the farmers' teams lined up for nearly a mile along Water Street and to the west, waiting to unload their straw for use in the manufacture of paper.

The company made paper bags, too, in buildings along First Street. The Western Paper Bag Company opened in 1882. It was one of the first manufacturers of square bottom bags. Some sources say the bags were invented in this factory; other sources say differently.

The factory made twenty different-sized grocery bags and paper flour sacks. Sixteen machines made 1,500,000 bags a day. The plant closed in 1900 when it became too expensive to ship wood pulp from the family's mills in Wisconsin after local lumber was used up.

The family did not limit its investments to Batavia. John's two sons, John M. and William S., entered the empire. In Appleton, Wisconsin, in 1873 a ground wood mill was organized, with William M. as a principal stockholder. He bought the company in 1876, and it operated with father John as its president and son William as vice-president. In 1881 William's younger brother John S. moved from Batavia to Appleton to look after the family's interests there.

In 1888 sons William and John established the vanNortwick Bank in Batavia and built the building at 12 West Wilson Street. By 1896 the bank was insolvent and was taken over by the second First National Bank of Batavia which is today's Harris Bank, Batavia.

In 1890 the vanNortwick Paper Company listed these businesses on its letterhead, all with offices on the second floor of their bank building[2]—vanNortwick Paper Company, Appleton Paper & Pulp Company, Kaukauna Paper Company, Combined Locks and Paper Company, Wisconsin Sulfite Fibre Company and Western Paper Bag Company.

William S. and John M. were in charge of the Appleton Manufacturing Company in Wisconsin. They made wind mills that competed with those of the U. S. W. E. and Pump Co.

In 1894 the men brought their business to Illinois and settled just north of Batavia between Fargo Boulevard and Fabyan Parkway. They built a company town named vanNortwick. Fire destroyed the plant six years later, and it was rebuilt in Batavia. One of those remaining buildings is now the Batavia Government Center.

In 1875 John moved his family to a farm on West Main Street. He had always loved fast horses, so he built a half-mile track and raced other Batavia men and their horses on Sunday afternoons.

When hard times hit again, John was forced to sell the farm. Years later when finances improved, he built a home across the street from the Congregational Church on Batavia Avenue. This house was used as part of the high school, built in 1914 on vanNortwick's land.

When John died, he was the wealthiest man in Kane County. He had come west with $3,000 in stocks and gold in 1836, financed his father and his sons, had gone broke more than once and still left an estate worth over $1,400,000, an immense sum in 1890.

Who better to tell the story of the old vanNortwick farmhouse than historian John Gustafson who lived there for many years. He wrote about his home on January 23, 1962. Additional data is added, but the description of the land and house is Mr. Gustafson's.[3]

The first land record is a patent dated March 10, 1843, whereby the United States granted to Horace Town 160 acres subject to the sale in the land office at Chicago.

The 160 acres were immediately divided, and Town and his wife Betsey sold 32 1/2 acres to vanNortwick, Barker, House & Co. The men apparently bought the land on speculation. They sold this first parcel for $40.62 or $1.25 an acre, showing no profit from the sale. During the next two years, the partners sold their shares to vanNortwick.

Shortly thereafter, the rear of the house was built. Verification of this is the date, October 1849, scribed with a stylus in the plaster of a cistern in the basement. Apparently vanNortwick built the original portion.

In November 1857 vanNortwick sold nine acres, the present size of the property to Captain Leonard J. Carr for $1,400 or $155.50 an acre. Not a bad profit in less than 15 years.

Sometime between 1857-75, the front part of the house was built by the captain. Born in Bangor, Maine, in 1807, Carr was a sea captain until 1839 when he came to Illinois and located on a farm at Nelson's Grove, 1 1/2 miles west of Batavia. In 1858 he moved to this farm and probably enlarged the house soon after, building the addition like a ship with a center hall upstairs and down with rooms off both sides. In 1995 adding to Gustafson's calculations, the back part of the home is 146 years old; the front part, 134.

In 1872 Carr moved into Batavia. In 1875 the house was deeded back to vanNortwick by Carr, then a widower, for $5,000 or $555.50 per acre. The value kept rising.

In 1911 the trustees of vanNortwick's estate sold the property to John and Frances Baker. When the Bakers retired and moved to town in 1918, the Gustafsons moved there from the northwest corner of McKee and Jefferson Streets. They purchased the property in 1928.

Nels Peter Gustafson was born in Sweden in 1854 and came to Big Rock in 1872. In 1887 he married Alice Butcher and the next year came to Batavia as a grocer. Later on this farm, he became a market gardener. Two of his girls, Nellie and Mary, married; but Alice, Lucile, John, and Arnold remained on the farm throughout their lifetimes. Alice taught in Batavia schools for forty years and has an elementary school named for her. Lucile was a history teacher in Ohio for many years. She and John became Batavia historians.

In 1963 Gustafson said, "The house stands solid as the Rock of Gibraltar, sincere and simple. The dimension timbers used in its construction are rough and full-sized. The oak timbers in the basement are hand-hewn. It contains three beautiful marble fireplaces, one, pure white, in the parlor."[4]

When the Gustafsons moved to the farm, the curved driveway reached to the front door; but that door was seldom used, and the driveway extension is gone. In 1918 there was a carriage shed attached to the house. When the Gustafsons had a picture window put in the dining room, the carpenter cut through rough sheathing an inch or more thick and twenty-one inches wide.

Downstairs the house has two large rooms in front, one on either side of the hall. The west room was the Gustafson's parlor; and the east room, their library. North of this is the dining room, a small kitchen that originally was a pantry, and a larger room that was the kitchen at one time. Upstairs there are five bedrooms, a bath, and a storage room in the rear.

This Italianate house was the second home to receive a Batavia Historical Society plaque.[5]

In 1995 the home is owned by L. A. and Sammie Maier King who live there with their two young sons. The Kings have restored the exterior of the house to colors of an earlier time.

---

[1] vanNortwick, 38 and 55.

[2] Stationery in the 1890s used by these companies lists their address as The Tribune Building. It is believed this is 12 West Wilson Street.

[3] From assorted notes of John Gustafson at the Depot Museum.

[4] From assorted notes of John Gustafson at the Depot Museum.

[5] Originally published February 6, 1991.

vanNortwick farm
later known as the Gustafson house

JOHN vanNORTWICK

Photos courtesy of the Batavia Historical Society

John vanNortwick residence
across from the Congregational Church
became part of the high school next door

William vanNortwick residence
south of his father's house
First Street and Batavia Avenue

JOHN BURNHAM
125 South Lincoln Street

The War of 1812 ended only a few months before John Burnham was born in 1816. As a youth in Vermont, John liked to study philosophical works, but economics made it necessary for him to help his father, who was a worker in gold and silver, a brass founder, and a coppersmith. Later he joined his father in the family's pump manufactory.

When he was thirty, John conceived the idea that wind could be harnessed to run pumps. He took his idea to Daniel Halladay who ran a machine shop. Halladay set to work to invent a self-regulating wind mill that would not break in severe winds. The two men formed a partnership to manufacture wind mills in Ellington, Connecticut. In 1857 Burnham came to Chicago to persuade John vanNortwick to use their wind mills to pump water for railroad engines. The three men formed a new company, the U. S. W. E. and Pump Co.

To house the new company, the men built stone buildings on the island along Water Street and shipped the machinery from the Halladay Wind Mill Company in Connecticut.

vanNortwick began as president of the new company as well as its general manager. Halladay was its superintendent, and Burnham was its general agent whose job it was to sell the mills. Later Burnham became the president.

When Daniel Halladay left Batavia for California in 1880, he gave Burnham credit for the success of their company. He said,

"Although I may justly feel that I have tried faithfully to discharge my duty to the company, yet I beg you are not to think me so vain as to desire more than a small share of the credit for the success of the company.

40

"I do not forget that Mr. Burnham suggested many years ago that a wind mill could be so constructed that it would be safe and self-controlled and so cheap as to come within the reach of the common farmer; many might be sold and thus a new industry be built.

"I shall not presume to tell you of the years of struggle that followed and how much of the success we finally achieved was due to the energy and perseverance of Mr. Burnham. Had it not been for his efforts, the modern wind mill would have been many years retarded in its introduction and use."[1]

John also invented a frost-proof tank to be used on railroads. It saved railroad companies millions of dollars.

The land on which the house where John, his wife Delia and children, William and Julia, lived was on more of John vanNortwick's early holdings. Thomas Cleveland, a cousin of U.S. President Grover Cleveland bought the land in 1852.

The house was built that year for Cleveland who came to Batavia in the early 1840s and ran a general store. From 1860-81, he was the station agent for the C. B. & Q. Railroad in Batavia.

In 1855 Cleveland sold the house to Thomas North, a Methodist minister. In 1856 the estate of Leonard Whiting obtained the house and in 1863 sold it to Burnham and Delia, whom he had married in 1846.

The Burnham family owned it until it was sold to Albert Burke in 1908. His daughter Mary, a Batavia art and history teacher, lived in the house until her death in 1952 when it was sold to the Clarence Kruger family. They lived in the house until Lyle and Terri Bergmann bought it in 1988.

The house is of Greek Revival architecture, frame with clapboard siding. The center section resembles the temple with wide pilasters drawing the viewers eye upward. Piers, representing Doric columns, support the roof of the temple section and on the one-story section act as the entrance.

Large dormer windows on the second story are topped by arches that have little pitched roofs looking like hats.

Bergmann has restored the balcony on the first floor extending across the east windows of the smaller parlor.

Greek Revival houses were painted white to resemble old Greek temples. Bergmann has instead painted this one Bennington grey with white trim.

There was a wind mill in the back yard to pump water and perhaps for Burnham to use for experiments.

Bergmann uncovered a flagstone walk that apparently led to a large stable that stood at the west end of the property.

The house has been enlarged and modernized over the years, but few changes have been made in the floor plan. Maps indicate that the south and west wings were added sometime between 1860 and 1890. The south wing included a library. The west wing included storage, a pantry, and an attached wood shed. The Bergmanns modernized the kitchen, and the west wing became part of the new kitchen.

A carriage door still exists in the north wing that allowed guests to enter directly into the summer parlor for dances. The string ensemble sat in an alcove off the parlor. A large hall which led from the alcove is now a bathroom.

The chimney of an unusual brick fireplace in the living room extends into the kitchen. This gives the kitchen an unique wall and indicates that perhaps it was not a part of the original house.

The enclosed staircase once lead straight to the three upstairs rooms directly from the front entrance. Today the bottom few steps curve into a side hall.

The Bergmanns restored the house and gardens to their former elegance, doing the work themselves. They used much of the original material except for the many square nails they removed. All the original floors still exist with beautiful parquet in the parlors and dining room. Contrary to today's style, but common in 1850, the studding is oak; but the woodwork is pine. Part of the basement still has a dirt floor.

The house is listed in the Library of Congress as a part of the Historic American Buildings Survey and has a Batavia Historical Society plaque at its front door.[2]

Burnham retired to California and died there in 1898.

---

[1] **Batavia Weekly News**, February 28, 1880.
[2] Originally published August 15, 1990.

John Burnham residence

DANIEL HALLADAY
432 Main Street

D aniel Halladay was born November 24, 1826, in Marlboro, Vermont, and married Susan W. Spooner at Ludlow, Massachusetts, in May 1849. They had a son who died in infancy and an adopted daughter.

Daniel was apprenticed as a machinist at Ludlow when he was nineteen years old. He was in charge of building machinery for the government's armory at Harpers Ferry, Virginia, by the time he was twenty-one.

He purchased an interest in the machine shops at Ellington, Connecticut, and here invented a self-governing wind engine which ranks as one of the most useful inventions of the era. He secured patents for several other inventions during this time.

There's a legend that says that when John Burnham suggested that Halladay invent a wind mill for pumping water in areas without flowing streams, Halladay answered, **"I can invent a self-regulating wind mill that will be safe from windstorms, but I don't know a single man who would want one."**

He did invent and patent the design, and he was right. No one in New England wanted it. Fortunately, John vanNortwick became interested and suggested Halladay move to the Midwest where he would be closer to the farmers who would buy his wind mills. When the U. S. W. E. & Pump Co. was formed, Halladay met with great success.

"The success of the company did not come immediately. It struggled through deep water for several years but finally pluck won the day, and the establishment became the largest of its kind in the country. Commencing with less than a half dozen workmen, employment grew until in 1883 the company

employed 180 men. The payroll for 1882 reached a total of $98,000.

"The business at first manufactured wind mills for pumping purposes. Finally their mill work ranged from the small 8 and 10 foot pumping mills to the 60-foot power mill. They also made pumps, feed grinders, railroad water tanks, and water pipes.

"The Halladay wind mill was a familiar sight in all the United States, its territories, the Sandwich Islands, Australia, New Zealand, Europe, Mexico and Canada"[1]

Daniel Halladay's home was on two lots of land that were sold by Denison K. Town to Charles A. Norris in 1857 for $200. This was part of 160 acres that Joseph Churchill owned on the west side of Batavia in 1841. He sold pieces of it to the Town brothers, Denison and Elijah.

In 1864 Norris sold one of the lots to Daniel for $1,200, indicating that a house had probably been built on it. Where Halladay lived in Batavia until he bought this house is not known.

The Halladays lived in the house until they moved to California. At that time they sold the house to Barton E. Sperry, a son of D. R., the founder of the foundry. After Barton died, the house was sold to James and Barbara Wertz. They sold it to Danny and LuAnn Bombard in 1983.

The house is of Greek Revival style and as such has the staircase right inside the front door and along an outside wall. There is a large entry way leading into the house "which rambles," according to LuAnn. In the entry way are photos of the Halladays. "They have come home," she said.

The interior has been remodeled perhaps more than once. Today there is a very large living room which was probably once a double parlor.

There is a bay window on the west wall of the living room which appears to have been added. A wonderful library with built-in book shelves has been added to the south of the living room. When the Sperrys left the house, their book collection stayed in the library. The Bombards still have the books on the shelves.

A large porch on the east has been glassed in to make a lovely sun room. There is also a closed-in back porch on the south side.

To the east of the living room and across the hallway is a dining room with a little mystery. Along the entire length of the east wall is an unusual alcove, four feet deep with a closet at the south end. What this might have been originally or whether it was added later is the mystery.

A large kitchen and a bathroom complete the first floor.

The Bombards have a blueprint that tells of a remodeling program on the second story in 1897. There are two stairways leading upstairs. At the top of the back one are a luggage room and two rooms that were labeled on a blueprint as servants' quarters. A hallway is designated as a sewing room and still has the wall of drawers and a work table that was used by a seamstress.

There is a master bedroom that once had an adjoining nursery. There are four bathrooms in the house.

Shutters adorn the front and sides of the house. At one time they were green but now are painted black. The exterior is white, but LuAnn guesses it may have once been a pale yellow.

Halladay retired in February 1880 and moved to California. At a farewell party he was given a gold watch with a vest chain and charm. The charm had his initials engraved on one side and a Halladay Standard Wind Mill engraved on the other.[2]

---

[1] **Aurora Beacon**, January 24, 1883.
[2] **Batavia Weekly News**, February 28, 1880.

Daniel Halladay residence

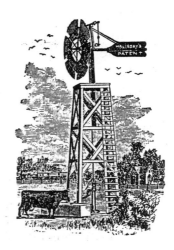

ALBERT WADSWORTH BULL
312 Spring Street

The first official record found of Albert Wadsworth Bull, a blacksmith, is the 1848 Batavia Township personal property tax roll. He was in Batavia prior to that time; however, because as early as May 1846, he is listed as a credit customer of C. A. Brooks & Company of Batavia, a general store.

The 1850 census reports that A. W. and his wife Emily were born in New York. A son Ivin was only a year old and was apparently born in Batavia. Bull is not listed in the 1857 Batavia Directory nor in the 1860 census. It's a guess that he was inadvertently omitted from these records.

By 1867 A. W. is again listed as a blacksmith and lives on the southeast corner of Spring and VanBuren streets. He was still in business in 1870 as he was charging at McGuire & Gregg's Blacksmith Shop. No other records of Ivin Bull can be found. Perhaps he died as an infant, or the census was wrong. Emily and A. W. did have a son George who never married. After Emily's death, A. W. married Lucy.

A. W. served on the Batavia village board for 7 one-year terms between 1858-71.

In 1854 A. W. bought land from Israel S. P. Lord and had a Greek Revival house of native limestone built. Limestone was used for the lintel above the front door and for window sills which were usually made of wood. The chimney was built of multi-colored fieldstone.

Previous owners of the land include Susannah Wilson and Alfred Churchill. Churchill, who once owned the entire block and had subdivided it, sold this lot to Lord.

After his father's death, George inherited the house, and in 1902 he sold it to Jed McNair, whose occupation is listed as a gardener in the 1924 city directory. In 1917 he was a First Ward alderman.

In 1929 McNair's estate sold the property to Glenn Crane, an undertaker and partner in the Crane & Swan Furniture Company located on the northeast corner of River and Wilson Streets.

In 1942 Crane sold the house to Davis Ewing who sold it to James Ford in 1957. Ford sold it to Charles Mitch who kept it three years before selling it to O. L. DeGraff. The DeGraffs owned the house until 1971 when they sold it to John Richards. Four years later he sold it to Ira and Judy Johnsen.

The original first floor now contains a bedroom and a very large living room. Evidence indicates that the living room may once have been two rooms. An addition, built of field stone, is today's kitchen, while the breakfast room was once a porch. The smallest of the three original second-floor bedrooms is now a bath.

The line of the original roof of shake shingles was changed when an addition was built. The windows are still the original six over six panes, common in the 1850s.

The exterior walls are fourteen inches thick as revealed by the door between today's living and dining rooms. A large piece of flagstone forms the threshold at this once exterior door. The old interior doors are unusual for they each have two full-length panels but no cross ones. Original latches remain on some of the interior doors.

The entry on the west was the front entrance until sometime between 1947-50. Until then the house's address was 54 VanBuren Street. Remnants of a driveway leading to this door were still in the yard when the Johnsens bought the house.

A milk bin is built into the north exterior wall, inside a porch. A Dutch door leads to the porch.

There is evidence that the beautiful winding staircase has been moved for it covers a corner of a window in a bath that was added under the stairs.

A very shallow closet at the bottom of the staircase has been made into book shelves by Johnsen.

Radiators heat the house as the old furnace is still in service. Beautiful hardwood floors cover wide pine sub-flooring. The floor joists still have bark on them. A trap door in the floor of a storage room is the entrance to the basement.

In the ivy-covered east wall is a wood storage bin about 15 inches deep with two 18-inch doors. The Johnsens have added a patio of brick from the old roundhouse in Aurora. At one edge of the patio is an old wrought iron fence they found in Wisconsin. "The lamb and willow tree design makes us think it is an old cemetery fence," said Judy.

There's a Greek Revival limestone garage which was probably built in the 1930s or 40s. Stone walls line the driveway, which along with the ivy, the patio, and lovely, big pine trees, give the yard the look of a country garden.[1]

---

[1] Originally published November 14, 1990.

A. W. Bull residence

GEORGE BASSETT
433 Main Street

The land on which this Greek Revival home sits was purchased from the government in 1841 by Joseph Churchill in the name of the eastern conglomerate. The partners sold out to John vanNortwick, who in 1855 sold the lots to George Bassett for $250.

Bassett was another New Yorker who came west and preempted a quarter section of land in Geneva Township. In 1848 he moved his family by team to Chicago and lived near the lake front for two years. He returned to Batavia and in 1856 built a simple house, the beginning of what it is today.

George was superintendent of bridges and buildings on the Chicago and North Western Railway. He built the first railroad station in Chicago, the old Canal Street Station.

He was also one of the nine charter members of the United States Wind Engine and Pump Company along with vanNortwick, Halladay, Burnham and others.

George was married to Harriet Humiston. Their son Nelson was a contractor and for a number of years was engaged in building government and other large buildings. From 1900-10 Nelson planned and did contract work on many factories in Batavia, including 2 of the Appleton buildings, 4 of the U. S. W. E. & Pump Co.'s, 2 large buildings for the Newton Wagon Company, and boiler rooms for Key and Chapell Dairy. He also constructed a 230-foot concrete dam in Batavia.[1]

In 1871 Bassett sold the house and land on Main Street to one of his daughters Mary, the wife of Peter Hobler. Hobler was the manager of the Chicago office of the Appleton Mfg. Co. while the plant was located in Appleton, Wisconsin. When the company built its new factory at vanNortwick in 1896, he was made general manager. Peter died just one month later; and Mary, six months later. The house was deeded to their daughter Harriet.

After Harriet died, David R. Sperry became its owner. Mr. and Mrs. Joseph A. Burnham acquired the house in 1955. Mr. Burnham was the Chairman of the Board and C.E.O. of Marshall Field & Company. After Mr. Burnham's death, Mrs. Burnham sold the home to Paul A. White who resides there today.

According to an account written by Mrs. Burnham in 1986, the house has undergone many changes through the years. A large porch was built for Mrs. Hobler as a wedding gift in 1900, but it was removed when Mrs. Sperry made a major transformation with the help of architect Frank Gray. An old photo shows that the wraparound porch extended from the west edge of the house to all but a few feet of the east edge. It extended back to the south wall of the east wing, now hidden by the sun room.

Mrs. Burnham states that the first indoor plumbing with a bathroom in Batavia was installed in this house, displacing one of the five bedrooms. At one time, the east portion was one-story, following the design of a mid-west Greek Revival farmhouse.

According to Burnham, the Sperrys formalized the facade with the pilaster-framed front entrance, added the sun porch and the brick porch floor, and divided an outside curved stairway. They added a modern kitchen wing and an attached garage after removing the summer kitchen and carriage barn. They created a large formal living room from a front and back parlor and built a fireplace and chimney in the new room. The house had been built without a fireplace as stoves had become popular in the 1850s.

The Burnhams added a keeping room with a flagstone floor east of the recently re-remodeled kitchen and created an apartment over the garage.

They installed the circular driveway of bricks from the Chicago stockyards. They transformed the sun room into a chestnut-paneled study. Today there are three bedrooms, a kitchen, family room, dining room, and office in the house.

Since the Whites have owned the home, they have made some changes to the interior. Again a new kitchen has been installed, and they redid the upstairs bathroom by adding a whirlpool tub. "It's a long way from a house with no plumbing to this," said the White's son, P. J. They also added the Palladian window in the apartment over the garage and built a second garage. They did extensive landscaping and added a mini-gazebo.

On the front of the house just under the roof line is a reproduction of a fire insurance plaque. These once showed that a home was insured so that the fire company would stop if the house were on fire. The house has been awarded a Batavia Historical Society plaque.[2]

---

[1] Thank you to Mary Peterson of Wheaton, a decendant of George Bassett, for sharing her research on the family and for her permission to use it here.

[2] Originally published March 6, 1991.

George Bassett residence

NELSON BURR
318 North VanBuren

Nelson Burr was born the year Christopher Payne first came to Head of Big Woods, 1833. He was raised on his father's farm in New York until he was seventeen years old. He had a natural gift for things mechanical, and his first job was manufacturing a patent fence which he expanded into a sash and door factory.

"I realize vividly the neglect of what might have been important events in my life. I always doubted if any good would come out of me, so I let many of my valuable mechanical constructions and devices go unnoticed. Later I would see others profiting from their use," Nelson once said.[1]

Nelson gained fame in 1857 when he came to Batavia and erected a mill to manufacture wooden pumps. This made him the first pump manufacturer in Illinois. In 1866 he established the Challenge Mill Company which later used the name Challenge Wind Mill & Feed Mill Company of Batavia, Illinois. It manufactured wind mills, feed mills, corn shellers, pumps, and other farm equipment.

Nelson finally patented one of his inventions, a metal grinding surface for grinding grain. He kept improving his invention until in 1869 it was used world wide. "My cotton seed hulling machine and my rice hulling machine also met with considerable success," Burr shyly admits.[2]

Nelson married Frances Fesler of New York in 1853. They had three children, Frances, Nellie, and Fannie. The girls were probably born in Batavia. Wife Frances died in 1863, and Nelson married Mrs. Christine Hapner of Ohio.

Burr owned considerable real estate in Batavia and Aurora as well as in Indiana and Michigan.

His home in Batavia was built in 1865 by Nelson about the time he married Christine. He purchased the land where the house sits from Israel S. P. Lord who had bought it from his brother-in-law Arthur and Emma Vanderveer in 1854 for $100. The land was once Isaac Wilson's and may have been a part of Christopher Payne's original claim.

Nelson used the house as $500 collateral in 1872 after the Challenge Company burned and had to be rebuilt. The plant suffered a total loss of $53,000, yet in thirty days it was rebuilt and manufacturing had resumed.

Burr died in 1913, and in 1919 Herbert and Leah Dailey purchased the house. In 1940 they sold it to Floyd and Marynell Anderson. In 1948 Paul and Natalie Seaman bought it and lived there until 1978 when they sold it to Casimir and Vickie Bied. The Bieds sold it in 1982 to Edward and Susan Mullinex, and in 1985 Clair and Deborah Penner bought the house.

An old photograph of the house at the Depot Museum identifies it as Italianate and shows ornate exterior trim that has been removed. There is still a belvedere, typical of the style.

The house sits on two lots with beautiful oak trees perhaps older than the house. A front porch has been removed, and a back porch has been enclosed to make a family room. Accounts of the house say that two or three chimneys have been removed, but the Penners can find no evidence that chimneys existed.

The Penners researched exterior color and found that the ones they have used, buff with museum white trim and green shutters, is appropriate to the time of the construction of the house. They stripped the old paint from the shutters. "One hundred twenty years of paint had destroyed all their detail," Mrs. Penner said, "and we wanted to see it." The house has a Batavia Historical Society plaque.

The Penners restored the interior to period colors. They have painted the walls museum white and the woodwork historic paint tones. Downstairs there is a living room, dining room, small kitchen, guest bedroom, sun room, huge screened porch, bath, closets, and storage. Upstairs are three bedrooms and a bath. There are beautiful oak floors throughout the house. In the living and dining rooms, the floor boards meet in a mitered corner pattern starting from a small square in the center of the room. A wood staircase with a carved banister dominates the entry hall. There are some leaded and stained glass windows.

"We love the historic background of our home and the challenges it presents," said Mrs. Penner. "Living in an old house changes your life style. We eat in a dining room; we cool off on the screen porch. It's a challenge to decorate with high ceilings and a floor plan that lets you stand anywhere and see all the rooms. It's a challenge to restore accurately, but comfortably, and we're still working on it." Mrs. Penner added.[3]

---

[1] BIOGRAPHICAL AND HISTORICAL RECORD, KANE COUNTY, ILLINOIS (Chicago: Beers, Leggett and Co. 1888) 492.

[2] BIOGRAPHICAL AND HISTORICAL RECORD 492.

[3] Originally published August 22, 1990.

Nelson Burr residence

DAVID R. SPERRY
33 South Jefferson Street

David Sperry was born in 1825 in New York where he married Marcia Edsal. David and Marcia had four children, Barton, Emma, Sarah, and Guy Rockwell. David engaged in farming in the East; but in 1868, he settled in Batavia. He built a foundry with A. N. Merrill, located at the corner of Wilson and Water Streets, which manufactured a line of farm boilers, kettles, and cookware. Later Sperry became the chief owner, and the firm became known as D. R. Sperry and Son.

Barton was a full partner with his father in the foundry. They were pioneers in the manufacture of fine ground hollowware, deep serving dishes made of silver.

In 1880 the Sperrys moved their foundry to North Aurora. It's still in operation under that name. After David's death in 1896, Barton became president of the company; and later his son, David Rockwell Sperry, succeeded him in the post.

D. R. Sperry and Company suffered several disasters. It burned down in 1885 and again in 1903. It was extensively damaged by a flood in 1887. Each time the Sperrys rebuilt.

The elder Sperrys lived at 505 First Street. The first record of their property is in August 1856 when John vanNortwick sold the land to Denison K. Town for $320. Two years later, Town sold the property to the widow of his brother Horace for $2,000. This indicates that a house had probably been added. This then is another of the homes built by D. K. Town. A legend says that the house was built around 1858, and it does appear on an 1860 map.

In 1864 the property was sold to Edward S. Smith, the postmaster, for $1,000. In 1868 the Smiths sold it to Sperry.

The home stayed in the Sperry family for over sixty years until in 1931 Hilmer and Amanda Johnson bought it. Hilmer was a carpenter/contractor. The house had been called "the Sperry House," but it eventually became the "Johnson House" for it was another fifty years before the current owners, Jack and Nancy Allen, bought it from the Johnson family.

The original part of the house remains. The Johnsons added a garage and stoop and tore off a south porch. They also remodeled the original staircase. The back two rooms on both floors appear to have been added, probably before 1926, according to Mrs. Allen. "The roof line appears on the insides of closets," she said.

One of the upstairs bedrooms has an unusual curved wall. It starts out one way and then expands the entire size of the room in the other direction. Mrs. Allen admits she doesn't know why. "It is almost as though it were anchored to a post or something to cause it to curve, or perhaps it was built that way to accommodate some piece of furniture," she said.

Three bedrooms and a bath are upstairs. Downstairs are a dining room, living room, kitchen, a small study, and a breakfast room. The Allens tore off the Johnson's garage and added a fireplace, the living room, a bedroom, a bath to the east, a porch and two-car garage on the north. Except for the fireplace and the remodeled staircase, the original house remains the same as it has been since 1858 as far as Mrs. Allen knows.

Two outstanding features of the exterior include the ten-foot bay window on the south and the east dormers with their original glass in the very old style of eight over eight panes.[1]

---

[1] Originally published January 23, 1991.

David R. Sperry residence

Charles W. Shumway residence

CHARLES W. SHUMWAY
HORATIO SHUMWAY
232 South Batavia Avenue

In 1995 the C. W. Shumway & Sons Foundry has operated for more than 120 years by Charles and his descendants. It's the oldest industry in Batavia. In 1988 the Batavia City Council renamed that part of Island Avenue from Wilson Street south to the foundry Shumway Avenue to honor the firm.

Charles W. was born in New York in 1827; and as a young man, he learned the tinner's trade. He came to Batavia in 1849 and ran a tin shop and hardware store at the corner of Batavia Avenue and First Street. All the goods he sold had to be purchased and shipped from New York.

In 1872 he met A. N. Merrill, and the men built a foundry on the island. Some of their earliest customers were those who needed material to rebuild Chicago after the great fire.

Many of the ornamental iron columns cast by the Shumway and Merrill Foundry grace some of Chicago's finest buildings such as the Palmer House, the Blackstone and LaSalle Hotels. The company also made castings used in the tunnels running under Chicago's State Street.

Eventually, Merrill retired, and Charles Osgood became a partner until his death in 1887. Later two of Shumway's sons, Horatio and Robert, became involved with the firm. Charles died in 1913.

Today's modern office with computer technology allows flexibility; moms need flexible on-the-job hours, and Attorney Mary Goblet believes in providing that flexibility.

For starters she uses Horatio Shumway's old home for an office. She moved into it in June of

1992, after purchasing it from Attorney Thomas Prindable who moved from the building after his office needs changed. "We are all learning to be flexible," said Goblet. "Our working arrangements and using this beautiful old home really make sense."

This parcel of land was first owned by Elijah Town who sold it to Denison Town in 1858. D. K., in turn, sold it to James Brown in 1866. Either Town or Brown built a house on the property sometime between 1860-92. The house is not shown on an 1860 map but is on an 1892 one. By 1872 Azro M. Spencer owned the property and did so until 1891 when Shumway bought it. He deeded it three months later to his son Horatio and his daughter-in-law Alice.

Horatio built the present house in 1914. It stayed in the family until 1983 when Prindable bought it from the Eunice Shumway estate.

It's dark brick, nearly square, and has three tiers, giving the appearance of a pyramid with its point cut off. The exterior with its large concrete front porch is a bit foreboding, but inside it is warm and comfortable.

Downstairs the center entrance opens into a hallway with narrow boarded hardwood floors which originally led to the kitchen and pantry area. Off the hallway were a parlor, living room, dining room, and kitchen. Today the parlor, with its brick fireplace, is the reception room; the living room is an office production area.

The dining room and kitchen were remodeled into offices. A smaller kitchen area and a downstairs powder room were made from the pantry area.

Upstairs are four bedrooms, all equipped as offices. The third floor, originally an attic, is a law library and conference room. It's accented by slanted roof lines, windows looking out onto Batavia Avenue and a glass conference table. One is struck by the flexibility and utility found in what was probably a dark attic used only for storage. Built-in bookcases filled with law books line the walls.

There are many large closets in the former bedrooms. Some have leaded glass windows that match the many windows throughout the house.

Prindable added walnut ceiling beams in the bedrooms to match those downstairs. He also added glass in the solid wood bedroom doors to provide more of an office look.[1]

---

[1] Originally published March 31, 1993.

Photo courtesy of the Batavia Historical Society

Osgood and Shumway Foundry

This picture was possibly taken prior to 1887 when Osgood died. His name would probably have been removed within a reasonable time after his death.

JOEL MCKEE
345 North Batavia Avenue

Joel McKee was born in Belfast in 1807 to Duncan and Mary Houston McKee. He was quite young when his family brought him to America. The family settled in Albany, and it was there Joel met James Risk. They came to Chicago by boat in 1834. They rode on a load of lumber to Batavia where they found Christopher Payne's family and few others.[1]

In Batavia in 1838, Joel married James' sister Jane. They had six children.

Joel's grandmother Sarah Houston soon joined her grandchildren. She died in May 1836 at age eighty-seven. She would have been eighty-five when she made the grueling journey from New York to the wilderness.

Brothers-in-law James, Joel, and Joel's brother Joseph claimed a great deal of land, including the slough that John vanNortwick got from Joel. Streets running through their property are named for the family. One is McKee Street, and the other, Houston Street after their mother.

Joel operated the first general store in the new settlement. It was built along the west side of the river at about Illinois Avenue. Joel eventually went into business with George B. Moss, and they bought vanNortwick's flouring mill on the east side of the river. It was described in 1866.

> "At the dam on the east side is found the old substantial flouring mill of McKee and Moss. The best brand of the establishment is a favorite on the Chicago Flour Exchange. Three run of stone are in constant use. The proprietors Joel McKee and George Moss are men who are favorably known both as capitalists, competent mechanics, and Christian gentlemen."[2]

With the mills, the men also bought water power the vanNortwicks had developed. An inventory of the land the partners owned was given at the time of Moss' death. They had a great deal along the east bank of the river from the dam south beyond Wilson Street, including one-half the river except for the water power sold to Howland and Co. for a paper mill and 66 feet of land and 400 square inches of water power sold to the Challenge Mill Co.[3]

Just before Moss died in 1872, the mill burned and was not rebuilt. A hundred yards south was a building the men erected for a pump manufactory. They apparently weren't successful as pump men for in 1866 Hugh Armstrong, a co-founder of the Challenge Wind Mill Company, manufactured stocking yarn in the building.

Joel lived on the west side of the river but had to go to the opposite side to work his mills each day. He grew tired of walking or riding a horse to Wilson Street to cross the bridge, so he built a foot bridge from his home to the mill. Unfortunately, it lasted only a short time before it was washed away. Joel died in 1873.

Joel's stately Italianate home is perched on a small hill overlooking North Batavia Avenue. It would once have looked over the river.

The hill and 160 acres of land surrounding it were first owned by Joel, who patented it from the government in 1841. It stayed in the McKee family until 1928 when Belle Cumming purchased it. Cumming sold it in 1936 to Nell W. Fabyan, whose estate sold it in 1941 to John Lane. He in turn sold it to Dr. Walter Grigg, who sold it in 1963 to its current owners, William and Elizabeth Hall.

McKee built the original section of the house, according to legend, in 1852. Originally, it was little more than a square, one-floor house built in pioneer style. This appears to be the back part of the house judging from the ceilings which are lower than those in the rest of the house.

As McKee prospered, he added to the house. There have been at least three additions, but the exact dates of these are lost.

The guest house was probably built around 1893. Hall found newspapers with that date inside the walls when he remodeled.

A legend says that John Dillinger rented the house shortly before he was killed in Chicago in 1934. The first month's rent was paid, but no one came to live in the house. When Dillinger's picture appeared in the paper after his death, Col. Fabyan knew to whom he had rented.[4]

Grigg screened in a porch and added a sun room. This necessitated a different back door.

The Halls did quite a bit of work on the house, but they have kept a careful balance between the old home and modern comforts.

They added a powder room, made an utility room from the old garage, and built a new garage.

A brick sidewalk leading to the front door is guarded by brick pillars, built by Hall's son, supporting twin lions. Gas lights adorn each side of the walk. From the walk, one sees the beautiful double door with its wrought iron screen and the second story balcony which serves as a roof above the door. Carved balustrades form a railing around the floor of the balcony which has a roof of its own. The Halls put a lighted Christmas tree on this balcony at holiday time.

There are matching bay windows, containing four windows each, balancing the front of the house and twin chimneys, all typical of the Italianate style.

As one enters the front door, the winding staircase with the carved newel posts and balustrades catches the eye. Coming in the back way, as most guests do, one is taken by the huge sun room to the south. The many windows bring the yard indoors.

To the north is a large library with an original fireplace with a wood, painted mantel. There is a formal living room with windows that would have once overlooked the river.

Upstairs there are four bedrooms with three bathrooms, a foyer, and a beautiful view of the river. A stairway leads to the attic and from there a staircase goes to the cupola which the Halls use only for decorating at Christmas. A back stairway winds into the kitchen.

Small back rooms upstairs were evidently once servants' quarters.

Hall's son built a large, brick patio which is surrounded by many rose bushes in the backyard. Trees buffer the noise from the highway. Being in the home or yard is like being in another time, and one can forget the highway is there.

The house has been plaqued by the Batavia Historical Society.[5]

---

[1] One wonders where the load of lumber was headed. If it were destined for Batavia, who ordered it?

[2] **Aurora Beacon**, May 10, 1866.

[3] Found in an agreement in the probate papers of George B. Moss.

[4] According to the story told by Col. Fabyan to Dr. Grigg and recorded in the notes of John Gustafson at the Depot Museum. Land records show that the Fabyans did not own the house until 1936. Dillinger was gunned down July 22, 1934.

[5] Originally published October 23, 1991.

Joel McKee residence

NATHAN S. YOUNG
106 N. VanBuren

Nathan Young was born in Vermont in 1818, the year Illinois became a state. He was one of seven children and went to school in Strafford. In 1840 he worked for a short time in Massachusetts. He returned to Strafford where he went into business selling dry goods, groceries, hardware, crockery, liquors, drugs, etc.

In the fall of 1843, Nathan settled in Sugar Grove, bringing his parents, brothers, and sisters. Fourteen years later he moved to Batavia and became a leading citizen of that village.

Nathan left a diary[1] in which he recorded life on the prairie. He tells what life was like for settlers in the Fox Valley in the 1840s. The chronicle of his first trip tells how Easterners traveled to the Fox River Valley.

Nathan came west to visit his brother Peleg who had staked a claim near Blackberry. Nathan wrote,

"Peleg had preempted 160 acres of prairie and broke up the same. In June 1843 he did 12 more acres and 20 acres on the Norris place where we lived for one year until November 5, 1844. Then we moved on to this 160 acres, where we built a house 24 x 30 in which we lived till October 1845 before it was plastered. Here we lived, Father, Mother, Peleg, George, me, Francis, and Marcella, until the spring of 1850, when everyone but Peleg and me moved 9 miles west to the Kaneville farm which we had bought from the U. S. at $1.25 per acre and built a good house thereon. I continued with Peleg on the old farm which had increased to 365 acres until the spring of 1852 when I sold out my half to Peleg and left."

The trip to Chicago took 11 days. **"I started out from Strafford on Monday, July 31, 1843, with my horse Tiger and a gig wagon at 6 a.m.,"** Young wrote.

He drove until night; started again at 6 a.m. and drove fifty miles to Troy, New York. It took until 4:30 p.m. The next morning he drove out two miles to leave Tiger and his wagon with a farmer.

At 5 p.m. he boarded a steamboat for Albany where he boarded a stagecoach for the two-hour ride to Schenectady. He immediately boarded a packet boat for Buffalo. After 4 days and 5 nights, on Sunday at 6 a.m., he arrived in Buffalo; five hours later, he got another steamboat for Chicago.

"We stopped at Detroit the next day for 8 hours, and I got to see the city," said Nathan. Three days later at 10 p.m. the boat landed at Chicago. At 5 p.m. he left on a load of lumber to visit his brother. It took fifty hours to arrive at P. Y. Bliss' Store in Sugar Grove Township.

Nathan stayed a week before he started back. Peleg accompanied him to Chicago, taking a load of wheat.

"On Monday, August 20, I took passage by steamboat for Buffalo. I backtracked my way, picked up my horse and wagon and arrived back in Strafford ten days later."

Nathan, his parents, and younger brothers and sisters began their preparation for the move to Illinois. On September 20, the 6 members of the family and 2,500 pounds of freight set out for Sugar Grove.

"The weather was terrible, rainy and misty all day, so we only got as far as Woodstock and put up for the night. The next day we crossed the mountain and stayed at Mindon over night. On the 22nd we drove within four miles of Whitehall and the next day took passage for Buffalo. The fare was $4 for each of the 5 and 1/2 passengers. Every 100 pounds of freight cost us 75 cents."

The next night, Sunday, the boat ran onto the stone abutments of a bridge, stove a hole in her bow; and she filled with water in five minutes.

"Because of the carelessness of the steersman, everything in the hold was wet. Only the trunks on

**deck were dry. It took us three hours to get every-
thing out on the shore,"** Nathan complained.

The next day all the passengers went to homes in Saratoga to find a room in which to dry their goods, but no one would accommodate them. Finally Mr. Holmes allowed fifty of them stay the night, including the Young family who camped in the corn barn. Nathan hauled the goods from the shore and unpacked them, wringing out the water and hanging them to dry. In the afternoon, he found a stove and pipe to put in the barn for warmth.

By Friday the boat was repaired. The rain stopped, and the passengers' goods were ready. They left Saratoga at 9 p.m. and for the next thirteen days had a rough ride. Many passengers suffered seasickness. When the boat docked in Milwaukee for a four-hour stop, the Youngs were happy to take a stroll.

The family arrived in Chicago at 6 a.m. on October 11. Nathan hired Mr. Smith to take the family to Sugar Grove, and they left immediately. When they arrived in Aurora, they stayed overnight at Smith's farm.

The next day the Young family arrived at their destination at 10 a.m. They took refuge with the Bliss family and stayed with them for four weeks. It had been twenty-two days since they had left Strafford, Vermont. Nathan turned right around with a wagon to return to Chicago for their goods. Three days later, after a difficult ride in an early snowstorm, he was back in Sugar Grove.

Nathan described his first week on the prairie.

**"Four days after I arrived back in Sugar Grove, I
took the windlass up to the new house, drawing
up gravel and dirt out of the well. I helped, Mr.
Bliss, too, by killing and dressing two pigs and pull-
ing turnips and digging potatoes. It warmed up so
I could haul wheat from the prairie farm with his
ox team.**

**"On Saturday I worked up at the new house
making laths which took me until Wednesday to**

finish. On that day Bliss helped me make mortar. As we worked we could see fires in all directions. On Saturday it was smoky from all the fires and cold, but Bliss and I made mortar, and Mr. Norris put it on the new house. We finished all in one day. We moved our goods by sleds up to Bliss's new house on the prairie."

The first week of November, Nathan split 159 rails on Peleg's land to make a yard for cattle. He pulled and piled chaff around the house for warmth. Later he stoned up the well, put up a gate post, dug a hole in the bottom of the cellar to put in sugar beets, turnips, and rutabagas and covered them with dirt. He spent the rest of 1843 working the farms with neighbors and preparing the house for the family.

When organization took place, Nathan was elected the first town clerk of Blackberry Township. In October 1852 he bought a farm 2 and 1/2 miles west of Batavia and planted 167 apple trees there.

Six years later he rented the yellow warehouse on the C. B. & Q. R. R. in Batavia, opening a grain store and lumber yard which he continued for five years. In 1859 he was elected supervisor of Batavia Township and re-elected for two terms. He filled the offices of highway commissioner, town assessor, collector and city treasurer, village trustee, and treasurer of the Congregational Church for twelve years.

After the lumber business, Young became a banker. In 1864, he was connected with the First National Bank of Batavia as a stockholder and director. He succeeded William Coffin as its president in 1878. The next year the bank liquidated and opened as the Coffin and Young Bank. On September 30, 1880, it was followed by the Bank of Gammon and Newton with Young serving as its first cashier until it, too, reorganized as the new First National Bank in November 1891. Nathan was this bank's vice president until 1901. Today this is the Harris Bank, Batavia.

Nathan was influential in other aspects of life in Batavia. He was one of the men who laid out the West Side Batavia Cemetery in April 1868 when it became a city cemetery.

He was a member of the East Batavia Board of Education for many years. In 1882 he was elected a member of the first Board of Library Directors, a position he held for fourteen years.

September 2, 1862, Nathan married Mary Hollister who came to Illinois in 1846 with her parents and settled on a farm three miles northeast of Batavia. Nathan and Mary had three children.

The Youngs bought the Monroe N. Lord house on State Street between VanBuren and Prairie in 1862. They lived there until 1893 when Nathan built a new house closer to the corner where they lived out their lives.

The land on which both of these houses were built was owned first by Isaac Wilson, then Lord, and finally Young.

The house is a large modified Queen Anne Style with seven peaked roofs adorned with a variety of shapes of shingles. It's painted blue with cream trim and has exterior doors which are painted an old barn red. It has a limestone foundation and is graced by an old-fashioned outside cellar door. The house today has an upstairs and a downstairs apartment and is rental property.

Leaded glass windows in the west wall of the third-floor attic and a round window in the east add beauty to the old home.

The somewhat small original front foyer is graced by a very beautifully carved Eastlake staircase. The newel post is exquisite. Pocket doors connect all of the downstairs rooms which now include a living room, kitchen, parlor, bedroom, and bath. A converted back stairs and landing have been made into a bedroom.

Upstairs there were originally five bedrooms, all with large closets. These can now be used as a living room, kitchen, and three bedrooms or as two bedrooms and a dining room. The upstairs landing for the back staircase has been made into a bathroom. All of these rooms have oversized windows.

The yard is reminiscent of the era in which the house was built. There are enormous oak trees on the east and south. Large evergreens are to the north. Overgrown bushes cover the crumbling cement sidewalks. Dandelions and a few wild flowers dot the lawn in the spring. Perhaps the trees weren't so large, and it was probably a wooden sidewalk, but one can imagine that the yard looked much the same when the Youngs moved into the house in 1893.

Nathan and Mary both died in 1907 and are buried in the West Batavia Cemetery.

---

[1] A copy of the original diary is in the archives at the Depot Museum.

Nathan S. Young residence

JUDGE SAMUEL D. LOCKWOOD

825 South Batavia Avenue

The fight against slavery in Illinois was led by a man who later became a revered citizen of Batavia. In 1853 Judge Samuel D. Lockwood moved his family here. Till then he had spent years working to abolish slavery in Illinois.

The first slaves were brought to Illinois in 1719. Philip Renault was employed to come to the territory to develop gold mines. He gathered 200 laborers and set sail from France. He stopped at Santa Domingo and purchased 500 black slaves. With these he sailed up the Mississippi River and established a headquarters near Kaskaskia. After twenty years of fruitless searching for gold, he sold his slaves to the French colonists.

The number of slaves in Illinois country increased very slowly. In 1763 when France ceded Illinois country to England, there were less than 1,000 slaves.

England did not interfere with slavery. After the revolution, Illinois country came into the United States with slavery firmly entrenched.

Congress passed the Ordinance of 1787 which prohibited slavery in the Northwest Territory. Gov. St. Clair said the Ordinance meant that no more slaves could be brought into the territory, but people could keep those they already had. Under this interpretation, slavery continued in Illinois even though Federal law forbade it.

Southern immigrants devised a plan to keep slaves in the territory. Negroes were brought in and bound out to service. In order that this kind of slavery might appear lawful, the Territorial Assembly passed a number of "black laws" in 1805-07, fixing the term of service, the rights and duties of masters, and further required that the names of black servants be registered with the county clerk where they lived.

When statehood became an issue, citizens took sides on the slavery question. Some wished to make Illinois a slave state—others felt that it was a moral evil and would hinder the settlement of the state. A third group wished to continue the "indenture system" because they feared that Congress would not admit Illinois with a slave constitution, and it would be better to compromise than to lose all. This faction won, and Congress accepted the Illinois constitution with the "indenture system" when Illinois became a state.

Later a pro-slavery element demanded a change in Illinois' constitution to make slavery legal. To do so, the people needed to pass a resolution calling for a constitutional convention.

In 1822 it was necessary to elect state and federal officers. The contest for governor was won by Edward Coles, an opponent of slavery. He stood alone in his cause for all other winners were in favor of slavery or at least weren't opposed to it.

At the time Lockwood was serving as Illinois states attorney, appointed by the general assembly of 1820-21. His appointment had taken 3 days and 45 ballots because of his antislavery stand.

To help him in the fight against slavery, Coles selected Lockwood as his Secretary of State, and the two men fought together in the cause of freedom.

The resolution for a new constitutional convention was proposed. After three bitter legislative votes, the resolution passed. The people would decide the issue. In August 1824, after a year and a half campaign, the voters defeated the resolution by 1,668 votes. Illinois would remain a free state.

In 1824 Lockwood was appointed an associate judge of the Illinois Supreme Court, a post he would hold until 1848. During his tenure, he won some antislavery decisions, but the "Black Laws" stayed on the statute books until 1865, long after he left the court.

By the time the first settlers came to Batavia, slavery had been officially outlawed in Illinois. The village founders were abolitionists and did not subscribe to the "indenture system."[1]

One of the homes most frequently mentioned in Batavia's history is Lockwood Hall, now the home of the John Gosselins. This Greek Revival home was built of native limestone in 1849 by Elijah Town.

The original government sale of the eighty acres which includes this land was to John Donnell in August 1841. Not long after, he sold some of it to Town. Town sold it to Lockwood in May, 1853. Lockwood sold parcels of the land until only 11 and 1/2 acres remained.

Lockwood was born in 1789 and came to Illinois in 1818. His job as a land agent for the Illinois Central Railroad brought him to Batavia. It was through the law that he became acquainted with Abraham Lincoln who practiced before him several times.

Lockwood died in 1874; and by that time, the Batavia property was in the names of his three daughters, Mary Coffin, Susan Porter, and Anna Merriman. By 1901 Porter sold the property to Caldwell Palmer. In 1906 Palmer sold it to Edward Hobler who in turn sold it two years later to Granville Johnston.

Johnston remodeled, making the north wing two-storied. In order to match the limestone, an old stone quarry had to be reopened.

Mr. and Mrs. George Council purchased the home after Mr. Johnston's death. Council farmed 250 acres near Bald Mound to support his wife and 10 children.

The Household Journal Company bought the house in 1917 from Mrs. Council. Rodney Brandon bought it in 1924. He was Vice President of the

D D D Corporation, Campana Corporation, and the Household Journal Company. He also served as an Illinois legislator and as the Superintendent of the Department of Public Welfare of Illinois for several years.

Brandon was a co-founder of Mooseheart and the executive secretary of the Loyal Order of the Moose. The Brandon family resided at Mooseheart until they purchased Lockwood Hall. Prior to 1924 the house had been made into apartments. Many people lived there according to Nancy Allen, Brandon's daughter.

Mrs. Brandon secured the aid of Mr. Abel in remodeling the house. He removed a wall and made a large library using some of the original walnut paneling to make new ones, one of which is a small secret hiding place. A fireplace fills a wall of the library. It's into this room that the Gosselin's visitors enter rather than through the original door.

A large dining room was made by removing another wall between the butler's pantry and a kitchen. A wall-sized butler's cupboard with leaded glass doors holds the Gosselin's dinnerware. The old summer kitchen is today's kitchen.

The original estate included the house, a barn built with wooden pegs, a smoke house, an ice house, and a sink carved out of limestone, according to an account written in 1963.

An earlier account states that Judge Lockwood's friends amusedly called the home Lockwood Castle because of its grandeur, but Mrs. Allen says that it was her mother who named it Lockwood Hall.

The Gosselins purchased the home in 1966. They made no changes in the structure of the house and have furnished it in period pieces.

The Brandon's crystal chandelier hangs above the dining table. Several large windows give an outdoor look. A short door leading to an outside pump supports the fact that this room was once the butler's pantry.

The door at the original main entrance, no longer used, with its beautiful leaded glass window, opens into an entry way which in turn opens into a large foyer leading to the beautiful walnut staircase with its one-inch square balustrades and square newel post. A window seat on the landing overlooks the west yard. A very small maid's room below the staircase is now a powder room. Mrs. Gosselin believes the stairway was widened by the Brandons as there appears to be a spot on the outside wall where a window was eliminated.

Old pictures of the home show two windows on the east wall, south of the main entrance, which made into three windows in the style of the day.

To the right of the entry way, a large living room welcomes visitors and leads into a sun room with exposed limestone walls. A terrace with a rose garden is reached through the sun room. The sun room was not a part of the original house as it does not show in early pictures, and a twenty-two-inch exterior wall is visible in the doorway between the living room and the sun room.

A feature of the master bedroom is the working pull chain toilet in the bathroom. Another of the upstairs bathrooms has an unusual shower. A ring of water comes straight down on a bather's head, and water shoots out of pipes aimed at the body. A third bathroom connects two more of the homes five bedrooms. If a bedroom doesn't have its own bathroom, it does have its own wash basin. The fifth bedroom leads to a back stairway. Each bedroom has at least one closet. Wall switches in the bedrooms are the old push-button type.

There are wonderful views from all the upstairs windows and porch. The attic has a number of windows for light and ventilation. Mrs. Gosselin calls them stomach windows because one has to lie on the stomach to see out of them.

One can almost see the carriages dropping off their passengers for a gala party under the portico, perhaps to greet the Lincolns if they did visit as legend says.

Brandon planted a half acre of peonies to the west of the house where other homes now face Jefferson Street. "The peonies were Brandon's hobby," said his daughter Nancy, "but we kids had to stand near the entrance of the cemetery and sell the peonies for a dollar a dozen to help keep the peony patch in shape."

There is a tale about two locust trees planted on the north side of the house as a memorial to Jefferson Davis and Abraham Lincoln who were both captains in the army during the Black Hawk War. One of the trees was lost in a storm. A Mr. Snow requested a piece of the wood for an Aurora Museum. When he questioned whose tree had come down, it was decided that Lincoln's was still standing. It's there today; its top held together with a chain.[2]

Motorists have grown accustomed to seeing a stately lady, riding her bicycle on South Batavia Avenue in Batavia. She is Cora Mae West, a secretary and poet, who has lived in Judge Lockwood's old barn for more than thirty years.

Cora grew up in Hardin County, Kentucky, and attended a separated county school two miles from home. In the summers she worked as a domestic six full days a week for $12.50. She then entered a high school which was financed by a Jewish gentleman for colored students.

After graduation she went to work full time as a domestic/baby sitter for the physician she had worked for during high school. The family moved to Carbondale, Illinois, and Cora went with them.

Cora worked for the doctor's family for a couple of years for almost no pay. She quit and worked as a domestic, cleaning houses for higher wages.

Finally she had enough money saved to start college, and she entered Southern Illinois University to take adult education courses.

Later she began a two-year course in nursing. Unfortunately, she had difficulty with chemistry, having had insufficient high school preparation, and she was unable to finish the program.

She took a job at the hospital in Carbondale, but again the pay was low so she moved on. She took and passed the state civil service nursing exams. She got a job at the Geneva Girls' School on Route 25 in June 1963 in the dispensary, working for Dr. O'Dwyer of Batavia as a registered nursing assistant.

When Cora began working at the school, she needed a place to live. She learned about the apartment in the barn at Lockwood Hall. If the Judge is looking down, he must be pleased that it is Cora living there.[3]

---

[1] Originally published February 2, 1994.
[2] Originally published in two parts, April 10 and 17, 1991.
[3] Condensed from an article originally published February 24, 1994.

Photo courtesy of the Batavia Historical Society

Lockwood Hall

RICHARD J. PATTERSON, M. D.
419 Union Avenue

Richard J. Patterson, born in 1817, was a native of Massachusetts. He graduated from Berkshire Medical College in 1842 and soon after received an appointment to the medical staff of the Ohio Lunatic Asylum at Columbus where he served for five years. He served five more years as the medical superintendent of the Indiana State Hospital for the Insane at Indianapolis and another five years as the medical superintendent of the Iowa State Hospital for the Insane.

In 1867 Patterson, along with his son John and his future son-in-law Seymour Wolcott, bought the defunct Batavia Institute and established a mental hospital for ladies of the middle class which he called Bellevue Place.

Dr. Patterson's wife Lucy was the hospital matron, and attendants and nurses completed his staff. In 1880 there were 17 patients and 17 staff members living at the hospital. In 1871 he added the two-story wings with the mansard roofs and increased his patient load from 25-30 women at a time.

An 1891 map shows 40,000 square feet of greenhouses to the west of the building. Stables and wagon sheds, a large laundry building with outside tanks for heating, two wind mills to pump water with a water tank, a smoke house and an ice house circled the building. Orchards and a vegetable garden provided a fresh supply of in-season food for the institution.

It was to this setting that Mary Todd Lincoln was sent in 1875. She arrived in Batavia by private train from Chicago accompanied by her son Robert on the ninety-minute ride. Mrs. Lincoln was here only three months before she left to live with her sister in Springfield.

It's possible that Bellevue was chosen for Mary's treatment because of Patterson's reputation as a doctor who believed in the simple treatment of rest, relaxation, and lax confinement. He was one of the first to believe that peace, quiet, and gentleness were beneficial to a cure of the mentally ill. The rural setting of Batavia fit those needs perfectly.

Patterson was well known as a professor at Chicago Medical College, and he kept an office in Chicago for the treatment of the mentally ill while maintaining Bellevue Place.

For a number of years the Pattersons lived in quarters on the first floor of the hospital. In 1886 they purchased the elegant home across Jefferson Street from the hospital. Dr. Patterson died in 1893, and Lucy, in 1911.

The house is a remarkable example of middle 19th century architecture. The limestone steps leading to the dull red double doors, the twin chimneys, the ornate brackets, and the cupola mark the Italianate style. Above the doors, which are accented with large brass fixtures, is a stained glass garden scene. Parquet floors in the living room, white woodwork and working fireplaces in the living room, library and master bedroom reflect 1880s architecture.

The land was first recorded in 1841 when Joseph Churchill of the eastern conglomerate bought it from the U. S. Land Office. D. K. Town eventually owned the entire block bounded by Jefferson Street, Batavia Avenue, Union Avenue and Elm Street. He sold E. H. Ferris, a sea captain, and his wife Eleanor that part along Jefferson Street extending from Union Avenue to Elm Street and east about three quarters of the block. Ferris built the west portion of the house with the cupola from Batavia limestone in 1863. It was finished in plaster with exquisite stone quoins. The vine-covered exterior walls are twenty-two inches thick as evidenced by an interior doorway.

In 1872 Ferris sold the property to Holbrook and Company of Chicago. Tom Holbrook moved into the house but died six months later. His widow and family remained there until 1886 when they sold it for $5,000 to Patterson.

Patterson built an addition on the east as large as the original house. It included two large rooms downstairs and two upstairs. A description of the house in 1920 says that it was rambling and not attractive to modern people. It had fourteen rooms on four lots; half of the land was an orchard. The house was valued at $6,000 and the land $4,000.[1]

Patterson lived in the house seven years. His heirs, members of the Wolcott family, lived there until 1929 when they sold it to Jay Barton. The Jaegers bought it from Barton in 1964.

A large entrance hall and 12-foot ceilings give a feeling of spaciousness. A simple wrought iron banister curves to the second floor. Barton replaced the original low, walnut banister for the sturdier iron one. As a small child who played with the Wolcott children, Lydia Jeane Stafney recalls, "It was easy and fun to slide down that low banister when Mrs. Wolcott wasn't looking."

The north wall of the dining room contains a country scene reminiscent of the 1880s painted by Eleanore Jaeger, a retired art teacher.

The living room is to the right in the newer portion of the house. It faces Union Avenue, one of the oldest, most historic streets in Batavia. A large, elegant bay window with an arched entrance makes a bright sitting area. The Jaegers found and restored a beautiful cherry fireplace behind a modern one in this room.

The morning room, with its eastern exposure, is a small but sun-filled area.

The remainder of the downstairs contains a library, with the original marble fireplace, a powder room, and a long narrow kitchen that was once the butler's pantry. Upstairs are four bedrooms with two half baths, a full bath, and two anterooms. Many of the windows have interior shutters.

The original house was built with a frame service wing, including a summer kitchen. Over this kitchen was a screened summer sleeping room. It had beds that hung from the ceiling. "We could swing on the beds," said Miss Stafney, "but only if we removed our shoes." In 1944 Barton moved this wing to the east edge of the property to 405 Union Avenue. One can compare the decorative brackets of the two houses.

The grounds add to the beauty of the home. A large carnelian cherry bush fills with color in the spring. Trees include those found in the Big Woods such as maple, tamarack, arbor vitae, buckeye, white pine, and hack berry. Spruce trees were planted by Captain Ferris from seedlings he brought from Norway.

A grassy patio can be reached through the dining room. To the north is a stone patio and garage.

A porch once led from the front of the house around the west side, but Barton removed it. "It was a charming porch," remembers Miss Stafney. A carriage house stood on the property at Elm Street, facing Jefferson. There was a clay tennis court with backstops on Elm Street. When Wolcott sold that part of the property, a grass tennis court was made east of the house. The boundary lines were cut with a lawn mower.

Legend says that Mrs. Lincoln visited the Patterson home. It could not have been in this house for she was at the hospital in 1875, and the Pattersons did not yet own it. Some say Mrs. Lincoln took her meals with the Pattersons. This she may have done, but it would had to have been in the hospital.[2]

---

[1] From inheritance tax papers of J. C. Patterson.
[2] Originally published February 20, 1991.

BATAVIA PLACES

Dr. Richard J. Pattrson residence

Seymour A. Wolcott residence

SEYMOUR A. WOLCOTT
345 Union Avenue

Seymour Wolcott was born in 1847 in New York. His parents brought him and his seven siblings to Batavia when he was seven years old. His father ran a general store on Batavia Avenue between First and Main Streets until the Civil War.

When the War began, Seymour enlisted with a number of other Batavia men and fought until its end. When the Batavia Chapter of the G. A. R. was formed, he became an active member.

After the war he returned to Batavia and opened a drug store for a time on South Batavia Avenue. He continued operating a pharmacy on the Island for many years even after he joined his future father-in-law in founding Bellevue Place.

Seymour returned to Batavia, New York, in 1871 to marry Caroline Olivia, the daughter of Dr. Patterson.

Seymour ran the pharmacy at the hospital and later managed the hospital as its secretary-treasurer and still later as its president. He was its president when he died, though his sons were really the ones managing it.

At the time of his death in an auto accident in Wisconsin in September 1940, he was ninety-three years old and the last of Batavia's Civil War sons. Richard Wolcott died in the crash with his father.

Caroline Olivia died in childbirth, and Seymour was married a second time to Mary Emerson from Maine.

The house where Seymour lived originally measured only 16 by 24 feet. Although it does not show on the 1860 plat map, H. F. Perkins rented the house for $40 that year, according to documents belonging to the Jack Allens.

The house is in that block Denison Town bought in 1856 from his brother. D. K. must have built the house, as he still owned this particular lot in 1866

when he sold it to E. H. Ferris, a tailor. Ferris kept it only three years before selling it to William Boyd for $500. Boyd sold it in 1872 to James Kelly, who sold it to Seymour Wolcott in 1876 for $2,500. The house remained in the Wolcott family until 1958 when the Allens purchased it.

The original house has been altered considerably to make it the classic example of Second (or French) Empire it is today. There is the mansard roof with dormer windows, one of which contains the paired panes characteristic of the style. The center dormer extends upward to form the usual tower which still has its iron cresting. There are typical matching bay windows on each side of the centered elegant entrance and another bay on the east. Shutters frame the windows. There are brackets about eighteen inches apart under the main roof, those of the bays, and that of the screened terrace.

Sometime between 1860-69 the house was extended to its present shape as evidenced by an 1869 aerial view. In 1876 in addition to the mansard roof with its tower, Wolcott added the second story over the original portion, the fancy woodwork, colored glass, and parquet floors. He was able to accomplish this with a $1,700 mortgage.

In 1948 Katherine Buchanan, a great niece of Wolcott's, built a large, two-level terrace in the back yard.

In 1970 the Allens roofed and screened the upper portion of the terrace. They adorned the screens with ornamental woodwork of an acorn and grape pattern. The screened terrace is reached through a Dutch door from the kitchen.

The interior of the house is spacious and gracefully decorated. The vestibule has gold floral and bird designs in its windows. The huge entrance hall shows off the beautiful Eastlake staircase with its carved newel post and balusters. The living room is the original section of the house containing the original fireplace. From an old door and an old newel post, the Allens made a woodwork frame for the fireplace. They inserted a window, high above the mantel with gold designs matching those found in the vestibule windows. The door, the post, and the extra window were all found on the property.

A dining room, kitchen, laundry/powder room, and a wood shed/mud room complete the downstairs. The mud room is primitive with its unfinished walls, a stark contrast to the beauty of the remainder of the house. Six bedrooms, a large hallway, and a bath are upstairs. This bath and the downstairs powder and laundry rooms appear to have been made from a back hallway and staircase. Throughout the house are the original pine floors except for the parquet in the bays.

The house has a Batavia Historical Society plaque showing it dates from 1860 and 1876. "I felt that was proper," Nancy Allen said. "The original house dates from 1860, but the house as it is today began in 1876."[1]

Mark Allen and his family now live in the house.

---

[1] Originally published January 30, 1991.

Dr. BERNARD J. CIGRAND

1184 South Batavia Avenue

Bernard Cigrand was born October 1, 1866, in Waubeka, Wisconsin. He was the youngest of six children of Nicholas and Susan Cigrand. Nicholas was a blacksmith and wagon maker.

Bernard taught at a country school, Stony Hill, in his home state, and it was there that he conceived the idea of observing June 14 as the "birthday of the flag." He chose that date because it was on June 14, 1777, that Congress officially adopted the Stars and Stripes as the flag of the United States.

He held the first observance of Flag Day in 1885 by assigning students to write themes on the American Flag. It was then that Bernard began his struggle to make Flag Day a national observance.

In 1894 Cigrand and a Civil War veteran, LeRoy VanHorn, led in establishing the American Flag Day Association in Chicago. This group held celebrations in Chicago parks; and because of the nationwide interest they aroused, the National American Flag Day Association was formed. Bernard became its president. Dr. Cigrand became known as the Father of Flag Day.

Cigrand's goal came closer to reality when President Woodrow Wilson on June 14, 1916, issued a proclamation calling for a nationwide observance of Flag Day. The observance didn't readily catch on. In 1927 President Coolidge issued a proclamation asking that June 14 be observed as national Flag Day, but it wasn't until August 3, 1949, that Congress finally gave its approval to a national celebration day.

In 1886 Bernard went to dental school and in 1912, he came to Batavia to practice dentistry. He left his practice to join the navy during World War I.

The land on which he built his Batavia home and dental office was purchased from William Grote and Alfred Carlisle. These gentlemen had many land holdings, but it was not determined from whom they purchased this particular large piece. Writings about Cigrand say he built the house in 1912, but county records show he bought the land in July 1913.

In 1920 Cigrand moved his dental offices to Aurora although he continued to live in Batavia until 1932 when he moved to Aurora. He died only weeks later. His house was sold to Norbert Tyrell, an attorney with a practice in Chicago.

In 1945 Tyrell's widow Mary sold the land to Chester Rehm, who ran an electric shop on Main Street. By 1950 Rehm had sold it to Horace Phipps, proprietor of Phipps Department Store, who in turn sold it to Dr. William C. Hallow, a clinical psychologist in 1965. Mrs. Hallow and her daughter Carol still live there.

The home is built of native limestone. Carol Hallow said that she had been told by a granddaughter of Cigrand that the limestone had been floated down river to the edge of the property and then pulled by horses up the hill to the building site. If this is true, a quarry would had to have been reopened as they were closed by that time.

On June 14, 1958, the Batavia American Legion Post dedicated a flag and flagpole at the house then owned by the Phipps family. Flag Day services were held around the pole each June 14 for a number of years.

The small house is unique because it has six fireplaces, one on the north and the south ends of each of three floors, including the basement. Some of the fireplaces have been boarded up or plastered over. The others have been converted to gas.

The three stories and the end fireplaces with their twin chimneys reflect the Federal style. A 1914 photograph of the home shows an entrance to a sun room that led into the basement. The room has been pulled away.

The house was built without electricity. The pipes for some of the gas lights are still visible. The house has hardwood maple floors and dark, wood beamed ceilings, typical of the Federal style. All the walls of the house are eighteen inches thick and of solid stone.

There are eight rooms in the house. Two were added by the Hallows for their offices. There is an eighteen-foot wide living room, a dining room, a kitchen, a very large foyer, and four bedrooms.

Dr. Cigrand's office was on the north end of the basement equipped with a foot-powered drill. When the Hallows removed a cabinet, one of Cigrand's business cards was found behind it.

To the north of the house is a row of large lilac bushes. In the back yard are shag bark, hickory, and oak trees, remnants of the old Big Woods.[1]

---

[1] Originally published June 5, 1991.

Dr. Bernard J. Cigrand residence and dental office

BLACK SETTLERS

Census records, obituaries, city directories, land, cemetery and probate records, and a paper read by Mrs. Jennie White Prince to the Batavia Historical Society in 1965[1] were used in researching this chapter. Prince gave only remembrances—some could be confirmed, most could not. The history of early black citizens is illusive. Many of their lives were only orally recorded.

The first official record of Blacks in Batavia is the 1860 census in which three families are listed. Since there are none in the 1850 Batavia census or the 1857 city directory, it appears that Blacks arrived in the late 1850s. However, James Stewart's obituary says he came to Batavia with his parents in 1852. If that is accurate, they may have been the first Black family to live in Batavia.

The Stewarts included William, a barber, born in North Carolina; Elizabeth, born in Indiana; their daughter Sarah, age 15, working as a serving girl; and sons Jordan, 13; and James, 11. Later Elizabeth's mother, Elizabeth Goings, who was born in 1751, lived with them.

The Stewart brothers joined the Union Army in 1864. Jordan was killed, but James returned to his father's barber shop on South Batavia Avenue to learn the trade he was to follow for over sixty years. After William's death, James opened a shop on the now vacant lot at 115 East Wilson Street. He bought the property in 1916 when there were two buildings on it. One, a frame home where the Stewarts lived, was at the back of the lot. The other, they rented out. After Amanda's death in 1939, the dilapidated buildings were sold and eventually razed.

James and Amanda celebrated their golden wedding anniversary in 1933, the year before James died. They had one daughter Gladys May, who died at age 3. They also had 3 sons, James Edward, Jr.; John William; and George McKinley, all of whom died before age 25.

James and Judith (Juda) Watts and three children are listed in the 1860 census. James, age 32, was a laborer born in Virginia. He was also a runaway slave. Juda was born in Missouri about 1833. Their children, William, age 13; Susan, age 2; and Lucinda, 8 months were all born in Illinois.

Watts lived on the northeast corner of River and Lake Streets in a log cabin. This was part of Joseph Lyon's original claim. Watts purchased two lots from Lyon in March 1859 for $100, possibly when he first came to Batavia. The property stayed in the Watts family until 1907 when heirs of James, Jr.'s, sold the property.

James, Sr., enlisted in the Union army and died in the Battle of Fredericksburg with the Army of Virginia. It was shortly after that in 1863 that James, Jr., was born.

Juda then married Robert Thurston. In the 1880 census she lives with Robert, their three children and a stepson, James Watts. James, Jr., died in 1913 and was survived by a wife, a son, and two sisters.

Later the Thurston girls, Carrie and Julia, lived in back of the Martena home on Lake Street. Carrie worked for the George Spooner family, and Julia worked for Dr. Annie Spencer as a dermatologist.

George Martena and his two boys and two girls lived opposite the Watts family. George, Jr., went west, came back and died here. Garfield was a polisher for the flat-iron company in Geneva. He played for dances and did some boxing on the side. No data other than Prince's was found on this family.

Steven Smith's family lived on Latham Street. According to the 1860 census, Steven was born in New York, was age 40, and worked as a laborer. His wife Susan was born in Missouri. They had 3 children, Samuel, age 17, a laborer; Jane, age 11; and Julia, 8. Smith's 1910 obituary reads, "He was a slave at the Kentucky plantations of Higenbotham and Oliver, families of wealth. Smith, born in Kentucky in 1811,[2] ran away from the

Higenbotham plantation and with the aid of the famous underground railroad escaped to Batavia where he resided for 50 years."

Prince's grandparents, John and Annie Ozier, lived on the east side of River Street at Gore Street, once the northernmost street in the village. In July 1905 they moved a block south, buying a lot for $100 from Sarah Chiles. The Oziers then lived directly north of the Watts.

Maria Hayes and her son Marshall, a painter, lived next door to the Oziers. Next door to them lived the Thurstons.

When Ozier came about 1869 to Batavia, there were eleven Black families here. Most had arrived seeking a home free from slavery and better working conditions. Many families lived on the east side in log cabins that are gone.

Thomas and Martha Ann Guyder lived on the west side on a five-acre farm in about the 1500 block of South Batavia Avenue. Land records show the Guyders were in Batavia as early as 1876. Thomas died in 1914; Martha, in 1903. The Guyders had children, Laura and Ray.

Others who lived on the west side included Robert Weaver, Lewis Smith, and John Brown. They lived together in 1880 in a home on Batavia Avenue. Weaver was a barber, Brown worked in one of the wind mill factories. Smith was a whitewasher. Katie Stewart lived at the home of John vanNortwick on Batavia Avenue and was that family's housekeeper. Her husband Willington was a servant in the same household.

Jerry and Lena White and family lived at the northwest corner of River and Latham. Over the years, White worked for the city, the Challenge Wind Mill Company, and the Creamery. He also hauled garbage, was a handyman and a gardener until blindness forced him to retire. White died in 1935 at age 89. Lena died in 1945.

John and Mary Jordan lived on the east side of River Street at Lake Street with their six children. In 1910 Mary still lived there. The boys were Charles; George, a janitor for the Aurora and Elgin Railroad at Wheaton; William, a handyman; and John. Daughter Amanda married James Stewart, and Elizabeth married Fred Gilbert.

William and Eva Caldwell lived two houses north of Logan Street on the west side of River Street. They both worked for Howells in Geneva, and Eva became one of the first female foremen there.

Mrs. Decorcey and her granddaughter Janey lived in the 200 block of North River Street.

Augustus "Dixie" Brown lived on North River Street. He was born in Virginia and was brought north by his employer. The first record of him in Batavia is in 1870 when he was nineteen years old. His obituary says that for twenty years he lived in and worked for the government in Washington. It doesn't say what years. Locally, he was a janitor at the U. S. W. E. & Pump Co., at the bank, and some of the stores. Mrs. Brown cleaned for the N. F. Rechards. Dixie died in 1919, leaving his wife but no children.

Reverend Abraham T. Hall lived on the east side on River Street. He came to Batavia in 1866 from Chicago after founding the Quinn Chapel, a large church on Wabash Avenue. He founded the African Methodist Episcopal Church in Batavia in 1865.[3]

He and his wife Joanna had eleven children, eight of whom grew to adulthood.

One son, Charles, went to Washington, DC, to work. He became well known for his work in the Census Bureau and was called the most important Washington Negro in the Roosevelt administration.

The rest of the children moved to Minnesota, New York, Pennsylvania, or Aurora.

Clabourn and Catherine Turner lived on Park Street in 1924 when she died. She belonged to the Episcopal Church. Clabourn died in 1928 at age 95. He was survived by his daughter, Rosa Jordan Slater (Mrs. George), who was the first Black female graduate of East Batavia High School. A city directory gives Turner's occupation as a market gardener, but he also worked as a janitor in the East Side School on Washington Avenue.

In 1880 James, Julia, and James, Jr., Turner lived on Spring Street. Whether they were related to Clabourn or not is unknown. They may have been related to Dixie Brown as he lived with them in 1870. James, Sr., was the foreman of the paint shop at the Challenge Company. He was a deacon in the African Methodist Church and superintendent of its Sunday School at the turn of the century. Another son, Albert, toured with a troupe of jubilee singers in the summer and assisted his father in the paint shop when he was home in the winter.[4]

James Buckner, a laborer, his wife Elizabeth, and son William lived next door to Clabourn in 1880 on Park Street. The Buckners were in Batavia in 1870. Next door to the Buckners was Theodore Hammond, a barber, and wife Kittie. Theodore's father Beverly lived a few houses away at Washington Avenue and Logan Street. Both Hammonds were veterans of the Civil War. All of the Hammonds had passed away before Beverly died in 1887.

Also living on Park Street in 1880 were William and Elizabeth Brown and daughter Frances. They were neighbors of Henry and Catherine Chapel and their children Ellen and John. Henry was a Civil War veteran, and both men worked at the Newton Wagon Company. Catherine kept a laundry and Ellen helped her mother there.

In 1880 James and Sarah Brown and their four children lived on Washington Avenue. James was a barber. A minister Stephen Jones and wife Lucy lived on the street, too.

Joshua Jackson lived on Church Street. He and his wife Jane had five children with them in 1880. Joshua and his son Charles were barbers.

Nero and Mary Norcross also lived on Church Street. They had 10 children with them in 1880. One was only

3 months old. Their oldest son, Charles, worked at the Newton Wagon Company. Nero died in 1889 at age 63.

---

[1] From the archival files at the Depot Museum.

[2] This disagrees with the census. If correct, Smith would have been 99 years old when he died. Census records place his birth about 1821-2. In the 1880 census a Stephen and Nancy Smith live on Washington Avenue. Stephen's occupation is given as minister, and he is the same age as the Steven in the 1860 census. Perhaps there were two Steven (Stephen) Smiths.

[3] **Past and Present of Kane County, Illinois**, 1878.

[4] **Aurora Daily Beacon**, January, 10, 1898.

Abraham ℱ Hall
Rosa May Jordan

Thomas ^his^ X *Guyden*
    mark

Photo courtesty of Batavia Historical Society

John and Anne Ozier in front of their residence

Photos courtesy of Batavia Historical Society

James Stewart residence and rental building

Watts residence--men are unidentified

SELBORNE
EDWIN, OLIVE, HARRIET HOLMES

1430 South Batavia Avenue

The land where *Villa Batavia* sits has had a number of owners since James Enos purchased it in a quarter section of land from the government in 1841. This would have cost him about $200.

In 1845 John and Sarah Buttrick bought the land for $2,000. This indicates that the house was probably built between 1841 and 1845 as is believed.

Others owned the land until after the turn of the century when it became part of the city and was subdivided. The house now occupies only seven acres of the original preemption.

Horace N. Jones, Lewis Burnett, Charles Deusner, and Sarah vanPelt each owned it for a time for the first twenty years of the 1900s. In October 1919 Sarah sold it to sisters, Harriet and Olive Holmes.[1]

These sisters had interesting lives. They were the daughters of Edwin and Jenny Holmes. The family was from Chicago and very wealthy. Edwin was in the lumber and mining business. The girls, along with their sister and brother, spent time in European schools. Jenny died in 1894, and Edwin met Susanna Emery.[2]

Susanna was a colorful and unconventional mining millionairess. She traveled around the world four times meeting kings, queens, a pope, and Edwin Holmes.

Mrs. Emery was known as Utah's Silver Queen. Susie, was born in Missouri in 1859. Her father owned land, a few slaves, and a general store in Richmond, Missouri. During the Civil War, he was commissioned a Captain in the Confederate Army. After the war, his property destroyed, he took his family to California hoping to strike it rich in gold mining. Instead he went bankrupt.

Susie found her way to Park City, Utah, where she met her first husband, Albion Emery. Together they invested in a silver mine that brought them wealth. Albion died ten years after they were married. Susie was grief stricken and traveled trying to get over her loss.

Sometime in 1895, after Jenny's death, Susie was introduced to Colonel Edwin Holmes. His title was not real, but he had served in the Union Army. When they met, Holmes' properties, lumber leases, and shipping interests on the Great Lakes were valued at $8 million. Thirteen years her senior, Holmes pursued Susie for four years. While the couple were dining with friends in New York, Edwin plucked a red rose from the table's centerpiece, tossed it to Susie and announced their marriage to the group. They were married October 12, 1899, in New York and went on a yearlong trip around the world.

On their return Edwin purchased a house for $40,000 in Salt Lake City that had once belonged to Brigham Young. He spent an additional $75,000 on renovations. The couple entertained lavishly, and their guest lists often included Utah's leading citizens.

Eventually Susie and Edwin left Utah and retired to Pasadena, California. Susie transformed a shake shingle two-story home into an impressive Tudor mansion valued at more than $1 million.

During the early 1920s, Utah's mining industries went through a major slump. Tensions developed between the couple as their mining dividends began to dwindle. They separated, and Edwin came to Batavia to live with Harriet and Olive at *Selborne*.

Susie was in Europe when Edwin died on September 31, 1925, at the age of eighty. She didn't return for his funeral but told the sisters to bury him in Chicago beside their mother.

Little is known about Edwin during his years in Batavia. It is suspected that he was ill most of that time. He died in Battle Creek, Michigan, perhaps at a family summer home. His residence is given as Batavia on his death records. From the settlement of his estate, it appears that his fortune had dwindled considerably.

Olive and Harriet were "real ladies" according to Don Schielke.[3] He remembers them from delivering groceries to the house as a young boy. It appears he may have known them as well as anyone, for they apparently did not socialize locally.

Harriet was a career woman, a graduate of Vassar who worked as a cancer researcher at the University of Chicago. She also taught at Northwestern University.

Olive stayed home and cared for the cats. Don remembers lots of cats. He delivered Richelieu Red Eye Alaskan Salmon each week for the animals. The ladies themselves ate only healthy foods—fruits and vegetables, never candies or fats.

"The women were tall, stately women who always dressed nicely," Don recalls. At Christmas Olive would tip him an extra $5.00, a large gift in depression years.

Olive told Don that they had found the farm when they had come to Batavia on one of the railroads' weekend excursion trips. They left Mill Creek Park on a walk toward town and saw it. It reminded them of a place in England they liked, and they bought it. They named it *Selborne* and registered the name in the recorder's office in Geneva.

Harriet wrote a description of their new home.[4]

THE BOOK OF SELBORNE FROM 1920
by Harriet Holmes

This place came into the possession of the present owners early in the year 1920 by purchase and was acquired by them for their permanent home. The price paid is not material to this history, nor is the exact description necessary more than to say that it lies along the Fox River, near Batavia, in Kane

County, Illinois, Section 27, Township 39, North of Range 8 East.

The little more than seven acres of this purchase, included the buildings of the "Old Homestead" consisting of an old farmhouse, a large barn, horse-barn, garden-house, chicken house and such sheds and out-houses as are usually found on an old place established fifty to seventy years ago. The framework of farm buildings of this period were almost universally of hand-hewed hard wood timber, and it was very much so in this instance, as when taking down the large barn which they had done, there was found solid oak sills, posts and even rafters.

In rebuilding the house, they retained what was suitable, which was mainly the front part which was really the oldest part and added only what was necessary to make a first-class two-story house for the greater part and with all modern improvements such as an up-to-date steam heating plant, an air pressure water system, hot and cold water all over the house, and an ample cistern with water piped into the other system.

The old horse-barn was retained for the present and answers for a tool house, work shop and general utility building, it having an attic room of ample size, also a basement story of the size of the whole building, all being well lighted with windows.

Selborne lies beautifully on the west bank of the Fox River, which along here has a number of small or moderate sized islands, some having full grown trees, others disappearing under water at the time of any great freshet. The prospective from this place to across the river and beyond is very fine and there is nothing out of harmony in the prospective. The land across the river is under a high state of cultivation and trees in the pasture land are quite symmetrical and are of a good healthy growth. A well-traveled highway is observable on that side of the river, and there is also a railroad which is a branch of the Burlington system over which trains occasionally pass.

On this *Selborne* side of the river there runs another railroad, belonging to the Chicago & North-Western system, and over this road many trains pass every day, it being on the "commuting" system out from Chicago, which is about forty miles directly east-ward from this point. Eight- and nine-car trains pass each way every day, and one and two car trains go at frequent intervals in the meantime during the day, but not late into the night which is fortunate. These short trains only go to the main line at Geneva, where their passengers are taken aboard other regular trains on the main line.

In front of the house at *Selborne* and about 100 feet distant from their front door passes every hour and half hour (afternoons) cars of the Chicago, Elgin & Aurora Electric road whose stop Number 11 is just in front of the front gate of *Selborne*. By taking one of these cars and going to Batavia, one mile northeast, and changing to the third rail electric, one can reach the "Big City" in an hour and twenty minutes by an Express train that makes few stops in the 40 miles and lands one within the "Loop" near Jackson Street. Other local trains take longer, but the service is good on all these trains and the regular steam-roads as well. The "Lincoln Highway" is the street in front of this place *Selborne*; and near there at Geneva, the "Roosevelt" highway goes out from Chicago and connects with that Trans-Continental highway, and it is an easy hour and a half run from Chicago to *Selborne* by automobile. So it will be seen that there is nothing lacking in the matter of transport so far as getting to and from *Selborne* is concerned.

The city of Aurora, six miles distant on the Electric road, is a lively town of over 40,000 inhabitants and has direct rail connection with Chicago over the Burlington system and the third rail Electric which has a branch to Batavia also.

Batavia itself is a town of not more than 2 or 3 thousand inhabitants,[5] but it has its churches, banks, stores, etc., much as any larger city. Still one would call it a sleepy old-fashioned sort of place. The present population are largely Swedish, and they are somewhat "clannish" as might naturally be expected. It is, however, a very pretty little place, and there is some manufacturing being done there; the largest plant being that of a wind mill company, that once did a rather large business in this class of work.

The natural slope of the land at *Selborne* gives good drainage to the soil, and an easy run-off of the surplus rainfall. The soil is mainly a rather stiff clay. At least it is stiff clay when it is dry as other times it is easily worked and brings good results in any reasonable sort of season. This land is understood to be somewhat sour, and needs an abundant supply of the right kind of fertilizer. There are about three acres of this land in alfalfa, and these parties plan to exchange this produce for animal manure and heavy labor which a farmer neighbor offers to furnish, thus relieving them of much trouble and expense. The underlying rock which is here quite near the surface, at least the lower portion of the place, is limestone and, of course, the drinking water on the place which comes from a deep well is hard water, but it is quite cold and entirely pure so far as its general quality is concerned.

Naturally being an old farm, the place was well stocked with weeds of which this party found no less that fifty-two varieties the first full year on the place. Some of these varieties of weeds were few, and some were not of the very worst kind, but all were bad enough and there were enough in quantity to make up for it as a whole. This party set about this eradication of weeds very systematically the season of 1921 and thought to eliminate not a few that year, but thought it would take at least five years to make the result very noticeable. Some of the very worst kinds were some of the noxious grasses, of which the quack grass was a specimen, another was the crab grass, knot grass, orchard grass all of which test the patience of any gardener. Other most noxious weeds are the mallow or cheese plant of which there is an immense quantity on the place. There are such quantities of dandelion which all know by sight, and how very difficult to eradicate.[6]

Olive died in the middle 1950s, and Harriet went into a nursing home in the late 1950s after selling the house to Rebecca May Simpson and her son John.

Nothing more of Harriet or Olive was found. It can be guessed that they, too, were returned to Chicago for burial.

The Simpsons lived in the house until 1984 when they sold it to Mark and Barbara Hoppe. The Hoppes sold it to its current owners, Richard Palmer and Fran Steiner, who operate the property as a bed and breakfast named *Villa Batavia*.

They rent Olive's and Harriet's old suites on the second floor to tourists. Olive's has a private bath, and Harriet's has a bedroom, bath and very large room that she used as a library and laboratory.

Of the buildings Harriet described, the barn, well house, and tool shed remain. There are still woods and a meadow where Richard has started a crop of evergreen trees.

On the first floor of the house are very formal dining and living rooms which are the original part of the house. Most of the house was once destroyed by fire, but the front wall is the original. There are French mantels of the 1700s in each of the oldest rooms.

There have been a number of decorating projects and four additions to the house over the years. A kitchen, library, and sun room were added in 1988. There is a large deck on the back facing the river and a large bay that can be used as a morning room. Bathrooms have been added and one very large one has been returned to an office.

The grounds are reminiscent of a past time. Brick and wooden sidewalks, a wraparound porch, flower beds, and the trees from the old big woods provide an oasis of green in the middle of the city along Route 31.

---

[1] Many thanks to Judy Dykman of Salt Lake City who directed me to the story of the Holmes family and gave permission to use some of her research in telling their story.

[2] Dykman is writing a biography of Susanna Bransford Emery Holmes Delitch Engalitcheff which will tell more about Edwin and his colorful life with Susanna.

[3] Donald Schielke is a native of Batavia and a charter member of the Senility Club. This small group of Batavia men meet weekly to discuss Batavia history.

[4] Thank you to Richard Palmer and Fran Steiner, owners of **Villa Batavia**, for sharing this **Story of Selborne** written by Harriet Holmes. They found the article when they moved into the house. They gave their permission for its use here.

5 Five thousand would have been more accurate.

[6] The original narrative contains an additional twenty-eight pages, cataloging the weeds found at *Selborne.*

Selborne

PAINTED LADIES

Painted ladies are buildings of many colors. Batavia has a number of these along her streets which add drama to the city's landscape. Because of the dedication of their owners, everyone enjoys their beauty.

223 South Jackson Street

This painted lady was built in 1852 according to owner Ray Bristow. If this is correct, it's likely that this is another home built by Denison Town. Thomas Cleveland owned the land before Town; but in 1852 he was building the Greek Revival house at 125 South Lincoln. Town sold the land to John McCasey in October 1858, and McCasey sold it the following month to John and Phebe Lyon who owned a livery stable. John sold the land to Joseph and Fanny Lyon three months later.

Col. Joseph Lyon was another settler from New York. His first claim was close to Christopher Payne's, and they built cabins near one another. It was on Joseph's claim that the first school in Head of Big Woods was erected. The men who excavated Payne's cabin in 1931 believed they found remnants of the school.

Lyon originally had a large claim which extended from about VanBuren Street to Batavia Avenue, north into Fabyan Forest Preserve and south to Wilson Street. One of his homes had to be moved to 17 North Jefferson Street[1] to make way for building the Methodist Church at 8 North Batavia Avenue in about 1887.

Joseph fought in the War of 1812. He arrived in Big Woods in April 1834 and stayed until 1875 when at the age of 84, he went to live with his children in California.

If Joseph built this house, then it had to have been built after 1860. In 1866 Joseph is listed as a farmer. He sold the land to Richard and Sarah

Branford in 1869. It was in the Branford family until Richard's granddaughter Kittie Branford sold it to Harry Larson in 1909.

Kittie's grandfather and father were farmers who came to Batavia in 1852. Kittie worked in the office of the U. S. W. E. & Pump Co. for many years.

The home was in the Larson family until 1952. It had several owners until in 1963 Bristow bought it. "Everyone identified our home as the 'Larson House' after we bought it," Bristow said.

The exterior color scheme is eye-catching. It's blue with cream trim and accents of colonial pink. There is a 4-section bay with curved glass at the top. Shutters with star cut outs are at all the windows.

Bristow has combined the modern with the old by adding a large, private deck complete with a hot tub in the back. A portion of the deck leads between two large old pine trees to an octagonal gazebo with screened walls.

It appears the interior has not changed a great deal. The white painted woodwork, common to the period, has been stripped, and the natural oak is seen. An original south porch has been enclosed and is a den heated by a "Standard 2" wood burning stove with the date 1893. There is no evidence of fireplaces.

Besides the den downstairs, there are a living room, dining room, kitchen, and a small room once used as a bedroom and now as a dressing and shower room for the hot tub. A window was converted to a door in order to reach the deck from this room. The dining room has a beautiful built-in hutch with leaded glass windows.

The upstairs was once one large area until walls were added. Now there are three bedrooms, a hallway, and a bath. All floors are narrow oak laths.

The back porch was obviously added because there is a sidewalk under it which probably led to an old outhouse.

There were two entrances to the partial basement—one from the outside and one from the kitchen. Bristow closed the one in the kitchen to make more room for modern appliances. The exterior entrance is now from the back porch.[2]

421 North Batavia Avenue

One very attractive painted lady stands at the corner of Maple Lane and North Batavia Avenue. She wears eight different colors or shades of colors, including three of dusty green and eggplant, with cream or black cherry accents, and belongs to Howard and Candace Broecker.

The house is a simplified Queen Anne. It has many features of the style—the eyebrow dormer, many gabled roofs, and the rounded bay window on the second floor extending above a rectangular triple bay on the first floor.

The first record of its land is the patent from the United States to James Risk in July 1841. Risk purchased the entire southwest quarter of Section 15 at the time. In November of 1841, he sold the southern portion to his brother-in-law Joel McKee.

The house was built in 1891[3] by a descendant of McKee, perhaps his son Emmet. A 1910 city directory shows E. McKee living in the house. City directories show that as late as 1940, Joel McKee, retired, occupied the house and was its owner.

From 1947-90, there was a succession of owners. Ralph Finley, a research engineer for Sears Roebuck in Chicago, owned the house for 13 years. The Benjamin Oswalts lived there another dozen years. The Tom Mairs lived in it for a short time. In 1977 James McAlpin bought it, and the Broeckers purchased it from the McAlpin family in 1990.

The interior of the home has had only a few changes since it was built. A screened porch on the south has become a family room. The northwest entrance has been closed, and that entry way is now a laundry room.

The house is reached from Batavia Avenue by a winding sidewalk. The porch is restored with steps leading from both the Avenue and Maple Lane sides, a common feature of Queen Anne porches. A garden greets the visitor from Maple Lane where the Broeckers added a circular gravel drive.

A winding staircase with two landings and square newel posts with unusual domed knobs dominates the large foyer.

There are a living room, dining room, large kitchen, morning room, four bedrooms, and two baths in the home, all decorated in the style and furnishing of the 1890s. Pocket doors can separate the living and dining rooms or the living room and the hallways.

Throughout the house are narrow lath hardwood floors except in the refurbished family room and kitchen where there is new white maple.

In the dining room is a fireplace rimmed with beautiful tiles. The hearth is of solid colored squares and the mantle is wooden. A nonworking, metal fireplace is in the master bedroom. Some original light fixtures remain upstairs and a silver plated old fixture hangs over the dining room table.

Beautiful wooden cabinets reach from floor to ceiling and cover the entire north wall of the kitchen. These appear to be original.

Maple and evergreen trees dot the yard and a lovely flagstone terrace can be seen from the family room eating area. The Broeckers enlarged the terrace, but it appears by the look of the stones that the original is very old. A deck was built on the south around a large, old tree. Occasionally the hole in the deck floor must be enlarged to accommodate the growth of the tree.[4]

9 South Batavia Avenue

This home is wooden and shows the variety of textures, projections, patterns, and asymmetry prominent in the Queen Anne style. The gable on the north has undercut soffits and great detailing. It's a fine example of the style.

The house was built in 1885 by Rev. Elijah H. Gammon, a Methodist minister turned manufacturer, just eleven years after the first Queen Anne home was built in America. He bought land that belonged to Levi Newton and George Clapp for his show place and moved three old buildings to make room for it.

On each side of a small stream that flowed across Batavia Avenue were two identical buildings. One was a post office during the Civil War and the other was a bank. One of these was moved to First Street and later destroyed. The other was moved to 125 South Batavia Avenue and has been replaced.[5] Clapp's old house is at 206 Union Avenue.

The house cost Gammon $27,000 to build, only $8,000 less than the Methodist Church he and his brother-in-law D. C. Newton built for the congregation across Batavia Avenue. Original drawings, framed and hung in the house, reveal that the architect was J. M. VanOsdel of Chicago.

In 1894 James P. Prindle, another Gammon brother-in-law, purchased the home from the Gammon Theological Seminary of Georgia to whom it had been willed.

At the time of Mrs. Prindle's death, the house was described as containing a hallway, parlor, library, dining room, butler's pantry, kitchen, tank room (housed the stove and ice box), cellar, and five bedrooms. There was also a bathroom upstairs and a rear hall.[6]

In 1917 Robert C. Hollister, a furniture dealer and funeral director, purchased it from the Prindle heirs. An article said, "This elegant, spacious and substantial structure will certainly make an ideal funeral home. The beautiful furnishings and draperies will be left and will help to make an attractive appearance. The house is in fine shape.

"The rooms are so well arranged that there can be an office, a show room, a reception hall and chapel on the main floor. The basement will be used for a work room, and a sanitary morgue will be installed. The upper floor will be used as a residence."[7]

About 1930 it became the Burnett and Johnson Funeral Home, and in the 1940s the Johnson Funeral Home. Joe Marconi bought it in 1977 and began renovation for a boutique.

Interior features include intricate, inlaid floors of walnut, mahogany, and cherry and the Italian mosaic floor of the vestibule. Shutters on the interior of windows roll up or down from the center so that ventilation and light can be easily controlled.

Seven fireplaces that heated the home all work. Some are beautifully hand-carved of Carrara marble and alabaster while others are of wood.

Each room contains detailed metal hinges and door knobs, stained glass windows and cherry paneling with square oak insets and beveled glass doors.

An Eastlake staircase is square paneled with a two-tiered railing and wainscoting. The landing contains a wall-sized window with several colored stained glass panels.

Marconi enlarged the south portion of the verandah which had already been enclosed and feels there has been a small addition on the north, but otherwise the structure is unchanged.

According to a blueprint, there was a front porch, a vestibule, a library, a dining room, a reception hall, a drawing room, a kitchen, a servants' dining room, a butler's pantry, and a pantry. The butler's pantry is now the dressing rooms, and the kitchen is the jewelry room. The other rooms are used for display. The north room contains an alcove that reveals what was once an arched door through which visitors entered the parlor from their carriage at a portico.

The Marconis live above the boutique. A sewing room is now the family kitchen. The second floor bedrooms have been turned into living areas.

One is a formal dining room with 1880s decor and furniture. There are also a large living room, a hall furnished with antiques, a library, and the master bedroom.

The attic has been divided into bedrooms and contains an entertainment area and the laundry room. The house seems even larger inside than outside. A large carriage house in the rear has been expanded and holds several shops.[8]

130 North Prairie

In 1852 Alfred Churchill sued his mother-in-law, Susanna Wilson, the widow of Isaac, to partition the block of land extending from Spring to State Street and from Prairie to Delia.

He won, and in 1856 he sold that land where this house sits to Dominic O'Boyle. Two years later, O'Boyle sold it to Mary Loftis.

Patrick Finley became its owner in 1863. He sold it to George D. Kenyon in 1866 for $143. In that year, George D. sold it to his son George R. for $500. Because the homestead right was waived at this time, it indicates that there was a house on the land. The tax assessor's records indicate that the house was built in 1870. In 1880 George R. Kenyon borrowed $3,000 to build an addition to the house. In the 1890s, George R. ran the North End Grocery at 515 North VanBuren Street, now the Mt. Victory Church of God in Christ.

George R. sold the house to Horace Jones, an attorney, in 1906. By 1923 Florence Marx owned it; and in 1925 Martin Turner was its owner.

In 1946 Arthur McConnaughay bought the house and in 1951 sold it to Francis Spiess. He sold it in 1955 to Thomas Kinney, Jr., and in 1978 the William McGraths purchased it.

The exterior of this Italianate house has been restored by the McGraths as nearly like the original as they could determine. It is buff stucco over clapboard with colonial red and blue trim. They have duplicated and replaced the spindles in the porch railing. Typical of the Italianate style, there are many brackets under the roof, and the main entrance has double doors. There is a gable roof line above the main entrance.

The doors at the front entrance were solid wood, but McGrath replaced them with stained glass panels and a transom. During the remodeling, he took up the threshold. Underneath was written "Kenyon House" in pencil. "It appeared to be the destination for a lumber delivery," said McGrath.

The structure of the original house has not been changed, and the addition can be easily identified because of the different foundations. The newer basement is deeper than the earlier part which is only five to six feet deep. It's probable, too, that the staircase was moved from just inside the front door to the center of the house. Interior doors were pocket ones, but they no longer work.

A large bay window dominates the south wall, and there was a screened porch on the back when the McGraths purchased the house. They added a doorway to the back, enlarged the porch, and added a deck.

Some windows are four over fours with arched upper panes, typical of the Italianate style. Others are the six over sixes. Ground floor windows reach from floor to ceiling. Because all the outside woodwork matches, the windows were apparently installed at the same time.

Remains of several chimneys for wood burning stoves were found. From their locations, it appears the original house had a living room, parlor or dining room, and a kitchen. The north wing with its exterior door is one-story. The rest is two-story. There are eleven and one-half foot ceilings downstairs and seven-foot ceilings upstairs.

Some attic space has been made into a modern-day loft while a walk-in attic space has been made into a second-floor utility room because there is no way to get into the basement from inside the house. The door to the utility room is the original board and batten with its original latch. A screened porch on the second floor has been added along with some closets. The maid's room was made into a large bath.

The old cistern with its three-foot long limestone cover remains in the backyard. Large pine and maple trees grace the front yard.[9]

135 South Lincoln

Another of Batavia's painted ladies watches over the northwest corner of Main and Lincoln Streets. Like others, it's in the Italianate style but has modern additions.

The land was some of that first owned by John vanNortwick. In 1850 he sold this piece to Harvey Reynolds who turned right around and sold it to Sackett Booth who owned it for twenty-five years.

By 1880 John Burnham owned the property, perhaps buying it because it adjoined his home to the north. His widow sold it to the Burke family apparently with the property to the north. In 1942 the Burke family sold this parcel to Frank Anderson who sold it four years later to Jerome Palecek. In 1948 John Weisner purchased it; and in the early 1990s, Mrs. Weisner sold it to Robert and Christine Ryba.

The house has many of the features of those built in the 1850s in Batavia. Its floors and fireplaces nearly match those in the home at 325 South Batavia Avenue built in 1858.

There was a small porch and a side entrance on the south. This was made into a forty-foot modern family room by the Weisners in the 1970s.

The house is entered from Lincoln Street into a very large hall with a beautiful winding, walnut staircase. There is a two-tiered railing which goes to the top of the stairs and across the head of the hallway.

The exterior door is a double one with two screens. The original brass doorknob is still there. The entry way has an oval stained glass window with an owl etched in its center. Mrs. Weisner had a beautiful marble and mirrored coat stand from the Don Carlos Newton home in the entry.

Off the entry is a library which may at one time have been used as a parlor. The dining room has a large bay to the south with a matching bay above it on the second story. There is also a bay window on the east.

The hard wood floors are bordered with parquet and the light fixtures appear to be the original ones. There are a number of closets throughout the house. In one of them is a marble wash stand. It's possible that the closet was built around the sink.

A very large kitchen with the original butler's pantry has built in cupboards reaching from floor to ceiling along one wall. The pantry leads into the dining room.

A large bathroom is located at the foot of the back staircase. It's so large that it may have been a maid's room at one time.

There are three black marble fireplaces in the house, one each in the library, dining room and master bedroom.

The Weisners made an attached sunken game room of the garage to the north over 20 years ago. This gave them room to raise their 5 children and a nephew. They lived in the house for 46 years. "It was a wonderful house for children," said Mrs. Weisner. "It was absolutely sound proof—we couldn't hear how noisy they were upstairs. There were many rooms and the children could have privacy with their friends."

Upstairs are four bedrooms and a sunken bathroom. What the bathroom was originally is unknown. It's possible from its location that it might have been a birthing room. The laundry room is upstairs in what was probably a maid or children's room.

The house sits on a limestone foundation on a large lot. Its decorative chimneys are rectangular and tiered and painted cream. The house is blue with white trim. The Ryba's have added gold accents.

There are several features that add to the beauty of the exterior. There are numerous brackets under the several roof lines. A circle window in the attic and an oval one at the east entrance enhance the house's charm. There is carved woodwork at all of the exteriors of the windows.

The Rybas are in the process of redecorating portions of the house and yard.

———————————

[1] Notes by John Gustafson at Depot Museum.
[2] Originally published August 4, 1993.
[3] According to records at the Depot Museum.
[4] Originally published January 27,1993.
[5] From assorted notes of John Gustafson at the Depot Museum.
[6] Probate papers, Mary C. Prindle.
[7] **Batavia Herald**, May 31, 1917.
[8] Originally published October 2, 1991.
[9] Originally published November 28, 1990.

223 South Jackson Street

130 North Prairie Street

421 North Batavia Avenue

135 South Lincoln Street

Phoro couresty Batavia Historical Society

9 South Batavia Avenue in an earlier day

118

PLACES OF MYSTERY

239 East Wilson Street

Some Batavia places are known for the mysteries they hold.

"I don't believe in ghosts or the supernatural, but this house is spiritual and mystical. It gives off a negative aura," said Carol Thuot-Leppert, who has owned this one and one-half story house since January 1989.

The land and house has had many owners and tenants since it was a part of Isaac Wilson's holdings. It has been a home, a doctor's office, an attorney's office, and a barbershop. Perhaps it's just tired.

In 1847 Emery Newton bought land, including this from Wilson. Newton, a tailor, came to Batavia before 1840 and lived here for many years.

Newton kept the land only one month before selling it to John Bellows who left Batavia soon after. Thompson Mead, Jr., bought the land at a sheriff's sale.

Exactly when the house was built isn't clear. The Batavia Historical Society dated it as of 1851 when it placed its first historical home plaque on it. Unfortunately, the records to substantiate the date are lost.

Bellows may have owned the land long enough to have built the house, but articles state it was erected for a member of the Mead family. They disagree as to which member.

Some accounts say it was the home of General Thompson Mead, Sr. However, an article written by Ora Mead, the general's granddaughter, states that he lived on land received from the government for his services in the War of 1812.[1] This land is now on the Fermilab Campus. The general, his wife, and two daughters of Thompson, Jr., are buried in Pioneer Cemetery on the old Mead farm.

It is likely that the house was built for Thompson, Jr., as it was he who owned the land. He's listed in the 1850 census as a physician and the owner of real estate worth $700. This amount indicates that a house was probably on his property at the time.

Mead's medical office was in the room that Leppert uses as a den. When repairing a wall of that room, she found a piece of beveled wood that was being used as a shim on which is painted "Dr. T. Mead, Batavia, Illinois."

Before that, however, Mead appears to have practiced on a site he rented from Israel Lord. He rented a portion of a "dwelling house" in March 1849 for a year at a rental fee of $26. He promised to keep the room in good condition and not to live there or use it to sell alcoholic liquors.[2]

In 1864 Clinton Mead, Thompson, Jr.'s son, sold the house to Oliver Wilcox who sold it to Israel Canfield the next year. Leppert made a dining room table from an old workbench she found in the cellar. Underneath is written Canfield Company, Lake Street, Chicago, Illinois.

Two years later, Canfield sold the house to Celestia Green; Green sold it to Sabrina Smith in 1876, and Smith sold it to Nathan S. Young. Young sold it in 1880 to Albert Tremain, and Tremain sold it to David P. Martin eight years later.

Martin sold it to John Burnett, a flour and feed merchant, in 1896. Mrs. Burnett, the former Frances Ballard, was a granddaughter of William van-Nortwick. In 1906 Jeanette Gronberg Joslyn became its owner.

Fred Simpson rented the house from 1917 until about 1923 when he bought it and sold it one month later to Ora Warner. Simpson and his wife Rose ran a grocery store across from the house on Wilson Street until about 1940.

In 1933 Herman Fischer became the owner of the house and used it as rental property. In 1938 Fischer sold it to Viva and Quentin Blewett who lived in it until their deaths in the 1960s. Quentin was an attorney and used the old doctor's office for his law practice.

Vernon Jefferson bought the house in 1970. Jefferson, who taught at the St. Charles Boys' School, lived in the house and ran Vern-on's El Capitan Barbershop in the back room that had been the dining room. In 1978 he sold the house to Mr. and Mrs. Gerald Skinner.

When the Skinners were restoring the dining room, they tore off the baseboard on the west wall. A partial skull, four pair of worn shoes, some lady's clothing, and other articles fell out.

Police sent the bones and clothing to laboratories for age analysis. The findings were inconclusive, but it was thought that the bones probably were of a sixteen- to eighteen-year old white female and were put in the wall about 1900.

Chemical analysis revealed that the bones were not of the sort that doctors used as specimen and that are occasionally found in old doctors' offices. They suggest a homicide. The clothes found in the wall were of a style predating 1900, and a 2-cent postage stamp found among the items was one printed only between 1883-87.

Leppert found another piece of Batavia history underneath layers of old wallpaper. A pencil written signature revealed that the first layer had been hung by Charles S. Robinson, paper hanger, April 2, 1904. Was he papering over the hidden skull?

The studs in the house are of solid white oak. The floors have no nails but are mortised and held together by wooden pegs.

Leppert found petrified wood in the attic. When she wanted new water pipes and telephone lines, workmen had great difficulty drilling through the wood. There's still bark on the oak beams.

There's little closet space, and the cellar is like a mine according to Leppert. She uses a small room at the back of the house for a pantry and storage.

The Blewetts had used it for a library. Its original use was probably as a summer kitchen.

Hollyhocks line the picket fence surrounding the house just as they probably always have. Petunias line the front walk, and there are boxes of blooming flowers on a garage wall that forms a pleasant back patio. Leppert has decorated in "contemporary country," and the six-room house is always warm and cozy despite its occasional negative history.[3]

121 Laurel Street

Denison Town bought land on the east side, too. The earliest recorded transaction of this piece is when Town sold it to Owen and Margaret Kavanaugh for $477 in 1876. The family owned the home for 77 years. Early maps show the house was built between 1860 and 69. It's likely Town built the house.

In 1867 Kavanaugh is identified as a quarryman who lives on the north side of Laurel Street between River Street and the railroad track.

Kavanaugh probably worked in the quarry just south of Laurel Street. They had six children. Three married and moved away. Margaret, Edward and Mary Ann remained in the house. Mary Ann was bedridden for many years. A neighborhood legend says that during her illness she had a vision of the Virgin Mary. Remembered accounts differ as to whether or not she was cured. She died before 1896 so accounts are only those handed down. Margaret was a clerk at the Fair Store in Chicago, and later she worked in one of the garment factories in Batavia.

Edward was the first paid policeman after Batavia incorporated in 1891. He had been a village constable several years before that. By 1893 his salary was $75 a month to run the one-man police force. He earned the title "rattle watch" because he nightly pulled on the doors of businesses to see if they were locked. He checked to see that city street lights burned each evening and rang the curfew bell when it was time for children to be home. His major problem was the "control of tramps, vagabonds, and vagrants who run wild about the city," according to early city records.[4] He was the first policeman to work out of the new city hall. He resigned in 1903 in an air of secrecy.

When Edward and Margaret moved to Aurora, the house was deeded to their married sister Ellen Heiss. She rented the property until she sold it to Waldo Hawxhurst in 1953. One lady who rented it during that time refused to go into the room in which the vision had supposedly taken place. "It was a haunted room," she said.

The Hawxhursts sold the home to George Maat in 1966, and he sold it to Laurence Baumgart in 1984. Baumgart sold it to Mary Ann and John Russ two years later.

The original two-story house was built in two offsetting squares so it's not a perfect rectangle. These rooms are the living room, den, dining room, and haunted room today.

Portieres made of beads separated the dining and living rooms in the 1910s and 20s according to neighbors who remember. By then a kitchen, sewing room, and a summer kitchen had been added. There were stained glass windows in the two bays. There is still an old Ben Franklin fireplace to which the Maats added Dutch tiles.

Neighbors remember large grape arbors, peach, apple, and black cherry trees. There was a large barn on the property in which a poor family was allowed to live for a time by the Kavanaughs.

Originally the house had no basement but a limestone foundation. Today's cellar is called a "dungeon" by the Russes. Just inside the back entrance was a trap door leading to the cellar. The original stairs are still there, but the Russes changed the entrance and removed the trap door.

The house has been added to and changed since 1953, but the original rooms and roof lines are intact. The haunted room is now a laundry room. Mrs. Russ explained, "I find I don't want to stay in the room too long, but I only had that feeling after hearing about the vision. Perhaps I just don't like doing laundry," she said.[5]

206 Union Avenue

This house was moved here by Elijah Gammon to make room for a home at 9 South Batavia Avenue.

Joel McKee sold land on Batavia Avenue to D. K. Town in 1842 for $63. In 1849 Town sold part of the land to George Clapp, a wagon maker, for $100. Clapp sold it thirty-six years later to Gammon for $400.

On an 1869 map the house is on Clapp's land on Batavia Avenue, but this isn't proof of when it was built or whether Clapp or Town built it. An 1885 map shows it was long and narrow, the same as the house on Union Avenue.

Gammon purchased the land on Union Avenue from Mary Porter of Racine in 1881. She had inherited the land from her mother, who had bought it from Henry Paddock thirteen years before.

Gammon sold the land to Sophia Peterson in May 1885, probably after he moved the house, suggesting it was moved sometime between March and May 1885. Peterson moved to San Francisco after selling the property to William Petrie of Evanston in 1887.

Petrie sold it to Francis Snow in 1892, and he sold it to Louis Hokonson in October 1899. The house remained in the Hokonson family until 1978. Gary and Mindy Lisewski bought it in 1984 and began restoring it.

Hokonson was Beverly Waterfield's grandfather, and she remembers the house. Its mystery is that two closets upstairs had solid wood jail doors. One had steel bars in an 8 x 8 inch opening. The other shows an equal-sized opening which was filled with wood. Waterfield said that a family legend says her grandfather bought the house from the city, and it was the first city hall and jail. Land records refute this, and there is no proof found. Hokonson bought the house from Snow. Where the jail doors came from cannot be proved, but it can be speculated.

A city jail can be accounted for except during the period when the first one was torn down during the Civil War and another was built in 1872 where the parking lot on First Street is today. Perhaps Clapp allowed the city to use his home as a jail during this time, but it doesn't seem likely. Nowhere is Clapp described as anything but a wagon maker or carpenter. He was never a justice of the peace or a police magistrate. If he'd been a jailer, some mention would surely have been given in records about him. It seems more likely that perhaps when the old jail was torn down in the early 1860s, Clapp did the job and took the doors home for his personal use. This theory can't be proven either. The mystery remains.

The original house apparently had two rooms downstairs separated by an opening with double doors. The hardware is still there, but the doors are not. Upstairs were three small bedrooms and the closets with the barred doors. Hokonson added a section to the back of the house containing a kitchen, a bedroom and what Waterfield calls a shanty. It was an unfinished room used for laundry and storage.

The cellar stairs are dovetailed. Hokonson dug part of the cellar by hand, carrying the dirt out in buckets. The cellar had many bins that Lisewski removed. Some were for coal for the immense furnace that has been replaced. It was the size of a small room and had to be removed in pieces. There are remains of a cistern in the cellar. Lisewski has found steel bars that fit one of the cellar windows— another unsolved mystery.

Floor beams still have bark on them. A few are trees with little hewing. The original floors seem to have been log, but beautiful hardwood now covers them.

A porch was added to the north and east sides. The outer walls are eighteen inches thick. The exterior is covered with cedar shingles, but underneath are narrow siding boards.[6]

1100 North Washington Avenue

It is unlikely that many today know of the ghosts who lived in the East Side Cemetery in the late 1840s. We are fortunate that in 1912, Nelson Burr related the story to the press.[7] According to Burr, a late night-traveler expected to see the ghosts. He learned of them from a man who had encountered them in the lonely hours between a Sunday evening and the dawn of Monday morning. In what year this sighting took place, Burr didn't make clear.

In early days, travel north and south through this area was along the east side of the river. The original plat of Batavia was laid on the east side in 1837, and there was no road on the west side until 1838. There were no burials in the cemetery until the middle of the 1840s. It was a privately owned cemetery, organized in 1845. There were earlier burials at 508 North Washington Avenue, but the bodies were moved when the East Side Cemetery began.

According to Burr, the ridge extending from the cemetery toward the river was more prominent than it was years later.

The early settlers to Kane County were mostly religious people. Some met to decide a place for building a church where they might worship. It was agreed to locate on a farm belonging to James Latham, a very early settler in Batavia.

Latham had built his home on the northeast corner of what is today Latham and VanBuren Streets. He was a warmhearted Christian and an enthusiastic Methodist who placed his house at the disposal of his Brethren for Christian friends in which they could hold services until their church was built.

Attending one of those Sunday evening services in Latham's home was a young lady who lived near Geneva. At the close of the service, young Adolphus Latham, James' son, escorted the lady home.

Returning on the crooked and rough path, he reached the burial ground about 3 a.m. He tried to whistle for courage but was too frightened. He set straight for home, looking neither right nor left and began to ascend the ridge. When he could see the crest of the ridge against the clear sky, his blood curdled. He saw an object on the ridge before him, rising from the earth by hitches, higher and higher. He stopped and saw distinctly the form of a man a half a length above the earth.

Adolphus ran as fast as he could, diagonally toward the river. The weird object ran along the same path, approaching him.

He ran first to the left, then to the right, through brush, over hills, behind trees until on the verge of collapse, Latham discovered he had somehow gained a slight advantage. At that moment, a strong, restless force came between him and the ghost, sending them in opposite directions.

Latham headed straight for home and was relieved to hear his dog barking. He went straight to bed and decided he'd not reveal that he had been in the vicinity of the graveyard so late on a Sunday night. He'd never tell the story and promised himself that it would never happen again. Still, he told the story to Mr. Burr.

At the end of that week, a young man appeared and told the Lathams he lived a few miles up river. He said that he had heard several reports about ghosts being seen in the graveyard and he wanted to tell his fearful experience with a score of ghosts he'd encountered a few evenings before.

The young stranger had been on the way home from a visit with family friends in Oswego. He had seen no ghosts on his way down river, but while he was neither a coward nor a believer in ghosts, he had intended to be past the graveyard before dark on his return home. Still visits being what they are, he didn't reach the cemetery until 3 a.m. on Sunday morning.

He looked around as he approached the ridge, and seeing nothing, started his ascent. When he reached the summit, he saw an object which seemed to be rising out of the ground. He stopped. The object rose no higher. He decided not to spend any time investigating. Instead, he hurried toward the river.

He didn't get far before he met another lively apparition. He changed direction and met another. He turned again and met still another. The ghosts kept getting thicker and more active. The woods and air seemed to be full of them. They appeared close enough to touch but passed quickly. Several times the stranger thought he smelled sulfur.

The young man said that this all occurred in a very short time; then the ghosts faded away. "It was no dream," he said. "When they were gone, I sped up the river a mile a minute."

Adolphus was very interested in the stranger's story. When it was finished, he said. "I've heard a great many stories about that ghost, but never heard of a Sunday night experience before. That was awful! I believe I could walk faster than you did to get away from a crowd like the one you met. You can bet I'll stay clear of any chances of being caught the way you were."[8]

---

[1] Found in notes of John Gustafson at Depot Museum.

[2] An agreement found in Dr. Mead's probate papers.

[3] Originally published in two installments, August 1 & 8, 1990.

[4] Village and city council meeting minutes of the 1880s and early 1890s.

[5] Originally published September 26, 1990.
[6] Originally published October 10, 1990.
[7] **Batavia Herald**, May 2, 1912.
[8] Originally published October 27, 1993.

239 East
Wilson
Street

206
Union
Avenue

121 Laurel Street

POTPOURRI

Potpourri means a collection of unrelated topics. The homes in this chapter do not have much in common. Some are located on what were once farms, others were always inside the city limits, and they are of different architectural styles.

403 McKee Street

This house was built on land originally belonging to Joseph Orr McKee. Joseph died a bachelor in 1859. The house stood on one-quarter of the block and had a number of outbuildings. The north side of McKee Street was farmland and a part of Joseph's estate when the house was apparently built in the 1860s.

In 1912 Emmett, Joel, and Jane McKee sold what was once their Uncle Joseph's land to Fannie Sterling who already owned adjoining property. Fannie sold it to Benjamin Anderson who farmed it. His widow Lillie sold it to Charles and Cecelia Buckingham. Charles was an employee of the General Electric X-ray Corporation in Chicago.

C. Willard Faltz purchased the home in 1954 and sold it two years later to Kenneth Eade who sold it to H. H. Chambers in 1962. Ten years later Chambers sold it to Jeff and Patricia Vidlak.

A large, beautiful stone patio that wraps around a huge Norwegian maple tree greets visitors as they approach the front entrance. Although the patio was built in 1945, it and the tree give an appearance of a step back into the 1800s and is a highlight of a visit to the house.

The yard is surrounded by a wooden picket fence that is of staggered heights. The top of the fence lowers as it nears Lincoln Street because when it was built, the city feared it would make it difficult for motorists to see at the corner. This concern provided a fence that is eye-catching and a real asset to the large yard.

The house has had few interior changes. Downstairs there are a living room, dining room, den, and kitchen. The den was apparently once a bedroom because it contains two closets. The kitchen has been enlarged. The large dining room has built-in china cabinets. There is simple, white woodwork throughout the house, typical of the rural farm house of the period.

Upstairs there are five rooms. The sun room was once probably used as a summer sleeping porch. Evidence in the ceiling and side walls of the master bedroom shows that it was once two rooms. One and one half baths have been added to the original floor plan.

There is a basement under the wing that runs east to west. This is the shape of the house on old maps and appears to be the original portion. The beams in the basement are very rough cut with single logs being used for the studs. There is a limestone foundation.

There are no fireplaces in the house, but a chimney rose through the center of the house where a stove would have been.

A neighbor told the Vidlaks that the house had wraparound porches at the turn of the century. There are French doors leading to a closed-in porch.

Amy Vidlak said of the house. "I was very little when we moved into this big, old house. We kids imagined it had ghosts though we never saw any. We'd lived in a little house. All this room was scary.[1]

420 McKee Street

The home of Russell and Adelaide Nelson was built in 1857. It was one of a hundred homes built by Batavia contractor John Benson.

The land was first owned by Joseph McKee. In 1857 McKee was a partner with his brother-in-law R. D. Smith, in a family supply store in Batavia.

McKee sold the land to blacksmith David and Betsey Lacy for $265 in 1856. Ten years later, Lacy sold it to Harvey and Ellen Conde Cole for $1,400. From these prices, it can be assumed that Lacy built the house.

In 1869 the First Methodist Church bought the home for a parsonage for $2,000. In 1905 the church sold it to John and Elizabeth Anderson, Russell's grandparents.

Exterior qualities of the house are those of the Greek Revival and Italianate styles. There are many brackets under the eaves and glass panels on the sides and atop the front door.

A beautiful entry welcomes one into the thirteen room home and is adorned with the original walnut staircase. There are a parlor, living room, dining room, two bedrooms, and kitchen on the first floor. Downstairs a bedroom was first a porch; another, a summer kitchen. Some of the windows have been changed. The woodwork is white. Bennington door knobs complete the white trim.

There are five rooms on the second floor which are used as a separate apartment. It was made around, but after, 1905.

In the backyard are large garages which were once barns and a chicken yard. A horse named Dick, who lived in the barn, was drafted by the army for service in World War I, according to Nelson. In 1911 Russell's father Martin began a plumbing business in the barns.

The house is plaqued by the Batavia Historical Society.[2]

503 McKee Street

This is another house built on Joel McKee's original land purchase. McKee apparently did not build it as he sold the land in 1856, and the house still doesn't show on maps as late as 1869.

Whether Thomas Cleveland built the house is not certain, but he may have. He purchased the land in 1856 when he moved from the house at 125 South Lincoln Street.

Like the McKees, Cleveland opened a general store in Batavia in 1840 though its location and how long he had the store isn't known. He was a C. B. & Q. station agent from 1860-81. He and his wife Olivia sold this land to John and Eveline Sheets in 1879. Four years later Sheets sold it to Mary Shumway who owned it until 1918 when she sold it to Julia Hurlburt. Hurlburt sold it to Mr. and Mrs. Gust Carlson five years later. They sold it to Anna Toohey, the widow of Thomas, and her mother Elizabeth Holscher, the next year.

Anna apparently married soon after for Anna Toohey Westberg and her husband sold the property to Harold and Martha Gustafson in 1927. Harold was employed at the Batavia Greenhouse Company. The Gustafsons sold the property to A. D. Murphy in 1983, and in 1989 Gary and Laura Rapp purchased it.

The house is an example of a prairie farm home. It's frame and was built in two squares like cubes with two stories. The Rapps restored the house, but with modern amenities. As they worked, they found improvements that took place through the generations. These are a history in themselves.

Going up the walk to the front entrance, one is taken by the curved eyebrow windows. A porch has been added and glassed in, but the two beautiful original doorways remain. They are side by side at right angles in the corner formed by the offsetting cubes. It's supposed that one of the doors led into the parlor for company and the other into the kitchen for the family. Today the parlor is the living room and the old kitchen, the dining room.

The Rapps dropped the ceiling and added wooden beams to support the second story. They took trim and plaster off the walls and found three layers of wallpaper used as sheeting. Either originally or in a previous restoration, 3/4 tongue and groove sheeting had been used, then wallpaper, and then plaster was added. This is unusual, according to Rapp, a carpenter, who did the restoration himself.

Another unusual feature Rapp found was that chimneys started on the second story. He had to remove them because of their weight. Obviously, the chimneys were for heating stoves on the second floor. Stoves would have been used as there were no fireplaces.

A bathroom was added in a long narrow room on the first floor that had obviously been a pantry. A depression is worn into the floor of the doorway to this room which one can imagine was made by a cook who stepped over the threshold into the room, stood, took an item from one of the shelves and turned to leave the room. Because the room was so narrow, her path would have always been the same, wearing away the wood.

When the Rapps bought the house, all the plumbing was exposed as it was added through the years. Rapp enclosed the pipes so they no longer show. Rapp estimates that he furnace and the heating pipes were probably installed in 1944. The electricity would have been added at some time.

There are three exterior walls in the present kitchen showing it was made from a back porch. The Rapps have been told this was done in 1929.

The staircase to the upstairs has been redone. There are three rooms upstairs and a half bath.

Large maple trees grow on a front lawn that is surrounded by a white wooden picket fence. The fence gives it the look of a farmhouse of the past century. The garage to the north is probably where the original barn stood.[3]

346 Elm Street

This house of three gables apparently was built by James Wood or Lois Marshall between 1874 and 1876. The house was owned and occupied by the

Doty family from February 1882 until July 1968 when it was purchased by Robert and Marcia Thorsen.

This was another house built on that block Denison Town bought in 1856. Town sold this parcel to James and Rosa Wood in 1874. Wood sold it to Lois Marshall in 1876, and Marshall sold it in 1882 to D. C. Newton, who immediately sold it to Fred Doty.

Fred went to work for the Newton Wagon Company in 1879 and worked there for eleven years. On May 3, 1882, he married Helen Burton and bought this house. Fred joined the staff of the U. S. W. E. & Pump Co. as an assistant secretary in 1890, the year he finished paying for the house.[4]

The house passed to their son Burton and then to his daughter Ruth, Mrs. Horace N. Jones. Mrs. Jones and their daughter Ruth sold it to the Thorsens.

No interior structural changes have been made, but a few have been made to the exterior. A picture taken in the early 1900s shows it very much as it looks today except that the four-windowed extended bay on the front has been changed to a picture window. In place of today's sun room on the southeast side is an open porch with a sidewalk leading to the front. Grape arbors extend from the porch into the spacious back yard. There is a hitching post at the edge of Elm Street which at the time was a dirt road.

A garage has been added, but when it would not hold a large car, a boot was built for the car's front end. Found in the garage is the front of a wooden crate addressed to F. H. Doty. The label shows it was a Wells Fargo shipment from Chicago.

Written on an interior garage wall is historical data. "October 1925, painted for $255. October 1934, painted for $100. Sleeping porch added in 1932." This porch is above the sun room that is believed to have been built in the 1920s.

Beside the garage is a very narrow room used as a tool shed. Mr. Doty was a builder and a tinkerer. The Thorsens found many handmade tools in this room which is almost too narrow to enter. In the limestone foundation near the room a door leads to a dirt-floored crawl space which was used to store lumber and tools, some of which remain.

In the cellar's limestone foundation is a metal-lined bin apparently to keep objects safe from fire. It's not a safe for valuables for it's not designed to lock.

The front entrance is a beautiful door with a transom. Downstairs are a living room, dining room, parlor, and kitchen. Four bedrooms and a bath are upstairs. Three of the bedrooms have doors opening onto porch roofs. The original summer kitchen is now the TV room.

There are narrow-boarded hardwood floors in many of the rooms, but the carpet in the parlor is an oriental one from the old Newton house at One North Batavia Avenue.

French doors between the parlor and the sun room have panes about six inches high with the muntins running only horizontally in the style of the 1920s. There are many windows throughout the house; most of which are very narrow. The windows all have exterior shutters. The house was apparently heated by stoves as there are no fireplaces.

In the backyard are a river stone patio and beautiful gardens with a sun dial and flowers that would have been growing at the time the house was built. These include Canterbury bells, sweet William, snap dragons, petunias, and day lilies.[5]

403 Elm Street

An 1860 map shows Lincoln Street[6] reaching Elm Street. This house is on the northwest corner. By 1871 the block of Lincoln, from Main to Elm, is labeled "Reserved Street." By 1892 the street is gone, and the house has a large east yard as it does today.

The house bears a Batavia Historical Society plaque, stating it was built in 1848. The first precise record found was in July, 1857, when George A. Blakeslee sold the land for $300 to Clement H. Goodwin, a lumber merchant, who was Blakeslee's partner in a number of land purchases in the early 1850s. Blakeslee and Goodwin were obviously engaged in farming as several mortgages for horses, wagons, and wheat were found.

It's not clear how Goodwin disposed of the land; but in January 1858, began a long line of mortgages, foreclosures, and deeds back and forth to such names as Sarah and Aaron Palmer, a reaper manufacturer; Mary and Solomon Trumble, a farmer; Mary Ann and Isaiah Griffin, who ran a hotel, a livery business, and was a partner with A. E. Davis in men's furnishings; W. W. Sterling; Emily M. Offensand; William vanNortwick; and Harvey McNair, a druggist. In 1888 it was deeded to Delia Burnham, Mrs. John Burnham.

Who of these lived in the house and who only held the deed through the mortgages and foreclosures is not certain. Many had residences elsewhere.

In 1894 the Burnhams sold the house to Andrew Otto Johnson, and its life settled down. It stayed in the Johnson family 100 years until 1985, when Sigred Johnson, Andrew's daughter, died; and the house was sold to Kimball C. Kleist. He kept it only two years before selling it to Harry and Barbara Taylor.

The Federal house is little changed from its original size and shape. It's rectangular, typical of the Federal style, and is built of frame and clapboard with a central chimney. The main entrance is in the gable end, another common Federal feature. This style was often used for rural homes.

At the front entrance, there was a huge limestone rock with steps carved into three sides. Dee Johnson Karas tells that her grandfather Andrew hated the three sided-stone; and sometime before

1929, tried to remove it and couldn't. After he damaged the rock, the current entrance roof and twin pillars were added. Concrete had to be poured to finish the small porch. The boulder remains. There was once also a huge black stone near the front entrance where horses were tied.

A side porch to the east remains, but the steps have been moved from the south end to the east side of the porch, and it has been screened.

Early pictures of the house show wooden sidewalks around it and a fence to the backyard. They also show a barn in the backyard.

A small, unheated room to the north was called the shanty, which was used for storing wood and produce from an enormous backyard garden. The pictures show a chimney in the north wall of the shanty, but Karas says she can't remember there being a stove or fireplace in the room. The Taylors converted the shanty into a family room.

Today the home has three bedrooms and a bath upstairs. There is a front parlor, living room, kitchen, and dining room downstairs. There is a beautiful front hall with an upstairs landing.

According to Karas, there was once a back staircase, too. As a young child she had fun running up one staircase and down the other while visiting her grandfather.[7]

120 North Washington Avenue

This home has been plaqued by the Batavia Historical Society. Records of land ownership, a copy of an old photograph, and early maps indicate that the house was built sometime in the late 1860s. Joseph and Carol Rundle purchased the home in 1964.

In August 1849 Alanson House sold the lots on which the house stands to John Waldron. George and Elvira Pierce bought it in 1855.

Pierce sold the land to James Lee who in turn sold it to James Yates in 1858. James' widow Anna sold the land to James Pierce, a machine tender at the vanNortwick paper mill, in 1867. Pierce sold the land to Theodore Wood, a partner with Frank Curtis in a grain and coal store at one of the depots, in 1869. Wood served in the Civil War and was at one time the president of the town board. The property stayed in the Wood family until the Rundles purchased it.

A house appears on the lot on an 1860 map, and an 1869 map shows a small one that runs east to west with a wing on the south side. Evidence of the missing wing exists in an exterior door in the dining room that Mrs. Rundle calls, "The door to nowhere."

The Rundles have a copy of an old photograph showing a house in the 1869 shape and some old glass slides of people standing in front of a house with a similar shape. Nothing is proven from the photos, but the shape of the 1869 house is found in today's house.

The house has been greatly enlarged. There are three large rooms, each behind another from west to east. The old photograph indicates that the middle section was probably the original house with the back and front sections added later. These rooms are the parlor, living room, and dining room. There are also a kitchen and bath downstairs. The upstairs has an identical floor plan with five bedrooms and a bath.

The kitchen had a large pantry and a butler's pantry which resembles a hallway between the kitchen and the dining room. Food was prepared in the kitchen and carried through the passageway into the dining room. Today this is all one pantry.

In the exterior wall near the pantry is an iceman's window. It opened from the bottom and was raised by the iceman who would push the block of ice through the wall without entering the house.

A beautiful bay window in the middle section gives further evidence that it is the original part of the house. This window has a copper roof, brackets, and dentils. The decoration is similar to several other houses on the east side, making Rundle believe that they were all built around the same time by the same builder. It seems there have been no other decorations on the house.

The original pine woodwork, horsehair plaster, and square, handmade nails remain in the entire house. The limestone foundation is twenty-four inches wide. There is a full attic with a rope and pulley window that can be opened for ventilation.

Stoves heated the home as there are no fireplaces. The chimney sat on a ledge on the first floor. There were two flues, one on the back side for the upstairs and the other for the cook stove in the kitchen.

The double exterior doors have a plaque on them inscribed, "G. Wood." This was for Gilbert Wood, a grandson of Theodore Wood, who in the 1940s was a state insurance examiner. However, it appears from the old photograph that the south doorway entering the center section is the original front door.

There were two large enclosed porches the entire width of the house on both floors on the east side. Each had 8 or 9 windows. The Rundles had to remove them when they deteriorated. At the Washington Avenue entrance is a hitching post that was cast at Shumway Foundry.

There are no trees on the property. There were once elm trees that succumbed to Dutch Elm disease. There was a very large white oak at the back corner of the house. "It was this tree that Gilbert Wood was trimming when he fell out, broke his neck, and died," said Rundle.

The east line of the Rundle's property was once the city limit line.[8]

637 North Batavia Avenue

Frank Lloyd Wright built this house north of the village in 1906. He named it *Ravine House* because of the natural slope of the land which he incorporated in its overall design.

In 1841 James Risk bought 160 acres of land from the government. He and subsequent owners sold the land piece by piece until the house now sits on only 2.3 acres.

Some other well-known owners of portions of the land were Joel McKee, Earl Newton, Josiah Towne, and Daniel Halladay. By the 1890s the Albert W. Gridley family owned the land. Accounts vary as to whether Albert W. or Logan Gridley had it built. Land records indicate that it was probably Logan, but his mother, Mrs. A. W., lived in it after her husband's death.

By 1912 the Gridleys had sold the house to Frank Snow, the president of the Challenge Feed Mill and Wind Mill Company. Members of the Snow family lived in the house until 1981.

The house has a living room, dining room, kitchen, family room, five bedrooms, two baths, two half baths, two rooms for servants' quarters, and a large verandah. There are three fireplaces made of Roman brick. The two-story house seems to rise beyond the verandah.

Wright became famous for his prairie style homes. They reflected the Midwestern prairie on which they were built. This house has his typical horizontal appearance with a pitched roof and thin, overhanging eaves. There are several large chimneys dotting the roof line. It is frame and buff stucco with brown oak trim inside and out, typical of the Wright style. On the second story, casement windows are arranged like a ribbon around the house and are tucked into the eaves.

According to an article written in 1961 by Frances Moran, Snow's daughter, this home was the first where Wright used the cantilever design. By extending the roof with the use of huge beams, he created a new, long, exaggerated feeling.

"He believed in bringing the outdoors indoors. Before Wright, no one had ever put windows at the corners of a house as they are on the ground floor of this one. By the use of sliding oak panel doors, the entire first floor may be separated into rooms or given a feeling of openness with the doors concealed in the walls."[9]

There is a barn on the property which dates to around 1890, but was moved to the spot, according to Mark Allen, who resided in the house in 1990. Moran's article indicated that Wright had built a barn on the property, but what has happened to it is not known.

This house is one of only four in Kane County on which the famous architect worked. One is in Aurora, and one is in Geneva. He also remodeled the second story of the Fabyan home in the Fabyan Forest Preserve.[10]

325 South Batavia Avenue/309 Union Avenue

This house is another located in that block owned by Denison Town in 1856 and is the home that is responsible for getting this author interested in writing about old houses while she lived there.

In January 1858 Town sold the two eastern lots on Union Avenue to Elijah H. Gammon for $800. On the lot nearest Batavia Avenue, Gammon built the front portion of today's house.

Gammon's house had features of a simplified Greek Revival. The front door with the interior staircase along the outside wall is particularly reminiscent of that style. The front door with its two side windows is also common in Greek Revival homes.

The house grew to the west as two additions were made. The first and a new roof line were added before the turn of the century. From Union Avenue it's easy to see where this addition was made because of the change in style of bay windows and exterior trim. A third addition was made in the late 1930s and serves today as a family room/sun room.

In 1863 Gammon sold the lot the house is on for $1,500 to E. Orville and Lemira Howland. This large increase in price is another confirmation that the house had been built by this time.

In November 1864 George B. Moss purchased the house. He didn't own it very long before he sold it to Enoch and Sarah Thomas. Enoch was a physician and very likely practiced medicine in the home. Dr. Thomas eventually bought the second lot from Gammon.

In 1874 James Prindle, a brother-in-law of Gammon, bought the house from Thomas. The Prindles lived there until April 1893 when they sold it to Cornelia Brown. The Brown heirs lived there until 1948 when it was purchased by Lloyd and Georgette Kautz. It eventually became known as the "Kautz House." In 1982 the Kautzes sold it to Jerry Harris.

There are fourteen rooms in the massive house, along with three bathrooms. The entrance on Batavia Avenue opens into a hallway leading into a kitchen that at one time may have been a library as evidenced by remnants of a servant's call box in a second-floor bedroom in the back half of the house.

This hall also opens into a very large, bright living room on the left which leads into a twin-sized dining room with a marble fireplace. The windows in these two rooms reach nearly from the fourteen foot ceiling to the floor.

Upstairs are three bedrooms, one of which has its own wash basin. A hallway has been walled to divide the house into two apartments. Three bedrooms in the west wing were originally off this same hallway. Two of those have their own wash basins.

BATAVIA PLACES

The house was apparently divided sometime between 1925 and 1928 when Edwin Brown owned it.

Downstairs in the west half there is a living room, dining room, kitchen, the sun room, and a bath.

This portion of the house carries the Union Avenue address. A large yard to the north, divided by flower gardens, a massive ginkgo tree and evergreens provide a spot of green space along South Batavia Avenue. There's a massive carriage house/barn in the rear, beside which the platform for the wind mill that once furnished water is still visible in the ground.

---

[1] Originally published March 18, 1992.

[2] Originally published February 19, 1992.

[3] Originally published May 20 1992.

[4] According to information in the possession of the Thorsens.

[5] Originally published August 14, 1990.

[6] Washington Street in 1860.

[7] Originally published March 27, 1991.

[8] Originally published November 20, 1991.

[9] Place of publication is unknown. It's a newspaper article, with no name of a paper, found in the vertical files at the Batavia Public Library.

[10] Originally published August 29, 1990.

346 Elm Street

325 South Batavia Avenue

403 Elm Street

403 McKee Street

420 McKee Street

637 North
Batavia
Avenue

503 McKee
Street

120 North Washington Avenue

Photo courtesy Windmill Herald

147

BUSINESS PLACES

vanNortwick Paper Company, 160 South Water Street

The home of the *Windmill Herald* was once one of the largest paper making factories in the country. It's one of several buildings that were in the vanNortwick Paper Manufacturing Company complex. About eighty persons worked there, making paper. It was one of the most successful mills in Illinois. At one time nearly all of the paper made there went to Chicago, much of it to publish the *Chicago Tribune*. It's fitting that a newspaper should be housed where once the largest amount of newsprint in the nation was made.

In the early days the vanNortwick dams made water power possible for factories on the banks of the river. The Fox River Manufacturing Company in 1851 saw this favorable manufacturing spot and built this stone building and fitted it with machinery to make railroad box cars. The owners, including Samuel D. Lockwood and his son-in-law, William Coffin, did not anticipate it would be too much for horses to haul the box cars uphill the half mile to the Chicago, Burlington and Quincy Railroad tracks. The plant lay idle for several years.

In 1862 the plant was purchased for $14,500 by Howland & Company, who fitted it for an extensive paper mill. Others investing in this project with Edgar and Edward Howland were James W. Harvey, Smith L. Mallory, John vanNortwick, Daniel Cornell, Joel McKee and George B. Moss. They operated with some success for about four years; but in 1866, it passed into the hands of Chicago Fiber & Paper Company. This firm operated a little more than a year until it was forced into bankruptcy.

In 1873 John vanNortwick bought the plant. With it he acquired two blocks of land which lay west of the river to Water Street and was bounded on the north by Wilson Street and on the south at about Elm Street. The description of the land reveals Batavia history.[1] It reads in part, "commencing on the west bank of the Fox River twenty-two rods north of Wilson Street, thence west to the east side of Mill Pond thence northerly and easterly along said Mill Pond to Fox River... Also commencing near the east side of said Mill Pond at a point of 6 rods north of the SE corner of the bridge over the Race at the Mill occupied by E. S. Town and Company... Also all of Block Five in the Assessors Second Addition in the Village of Batavia. The Boundary of said block being a line equally distant from the Race at saw mill and the Race on said Block Five. Also the water rights and privileges conveyed by John vanNortwick to the Batavia Manufacturing Company[2] on April 6, 1857...."

Today the building is in the center of three adjoining ones. It's built of native cut stone, is two stories high, with a basement and is 150 feet long. An early article described the building.[3] "The mills occupy a large substantial stone building or rather series of buildings, three stories high, sitting directly on the bank of the Fox River from which an abundant water power is obtained. These mills are equipped with complete and the latest improved machinery. In addition to the water power, this mill has a complete steam engine plant so that the mills can be operated by steam alone when necessary."

Water power was available not only because of the dams, but because vanNortwick had dredged the marsh he had acquired in trade from Joel McKee at Wilson and Water Streets and had directed the water under First Street into his factory to run his turbines. The water exited the building back into the river.

An 1885 map shows that coal sheds and a lime house were attached to the front of the building. There are remnants of railroad tracks inside the building showing that at one time shipping was done out of it.

In 1897 the property was turned over to a trust for the vanNortwick heirs, and in 1901 was sold to the U. S. W. E. and Pump Co. which had started across First Street in 1863 to manufacture Halladay wind mills. The company used the building as a warehouse according to a 1904 map.

During World War II the building was part of Batavia Metal Products, Inc., owned by Dr. Henry Garsson and his partners. This company had an outstanding record in the production of carloads of essential war equipment used in both the European and Japanese Campaigns. Still, its owners went to prison after the war for defrauding the government.

Production was round the clock. Mortar shells were made in this building and then filled with powder in a building to the east. On the second story of the building were showers and a workers' cafeteria according to Dan Stellato, Vice-President of Batavia Enterprises who bought the complex in 1959.

Since then others who have used parts of the buildings over the years have been Flinn Scientific, Batavia Enterprises, Corrugated Interpacking, Parmarco, and Batavia Container. The *Windmill Herald* moved into the building in October 1990.

Extensive remodeling to fit each tenant's use has altered the interior many times. Blocked up windows and doors and overhead tracks are evidence of previous residents' uses. One can stand in the vast unoccupied space and imagine the paper making machines, the lime vats, the rag bins, and the old turbines run by the power of the Fox River.[4]

28 Water Street

When John Burnham, John vanNortwick, and others formed the United States Wind Engine and Pump Co. in 1847 to manufacture Daniel Halladay's wind mills, they built limestone buildings on land owned by vanNortwick.

One of those new buildings is today known as the Tower Business Center and is owned by Batavia Enterprises.

The exterior of the building was much as it is today, three stories high and made of Batavia limestone. The wind mill company used the first floor for packaging, the second floor for an office and pattern shop, and the third floor as its paint shop. The pattern shop contained a jig saw, a rip saw, and a wood lathe.

Attached to the back of the building was the iron and lumber shed which appears to have been added after 1871. Marks on the north side of the tower indicate that another structure was once attached, and apparently it was this shed. The tower had a water tank on its roof.

In 1942 Batavia Metal Products took over all the buildings of the U. S. W. E. & P. Co. as part of its complex for manufacturing war materials. The exterior of the building has been improved with a new roof on the tower and modern canopies above the entrances. The interior has been renovated to provide a variety of office sizes and designs.[5]

2 and 4 North Batavia Avenue

After the Chicago fire of 1871, the Swedish population in Batavia grew rapidly. The first business venture of the Swedes in Batavia was a clothing store. Ten men each subscribed one dollar to finance the venture, but it didn't last long. The number of stockholders was soon reduced to Oscar and John A. Anderson, who were, what else, brothers-in-law.

The men built a wooden building on the northeast corner of Batavia Avenue and Wilson Street on land that once was a part of Col. Joseph Lyon's claim. In June 1872 they were advertising for tenants for their new building.

In about 1892, the frame building was moved to 613 & 615 Houston Street to be used as a storehouse for flour. Today it's an apartment house.

The men then built the imposing brick and stone block that still stands at the original corner. It's a beautiful and substantial structure, 50 feet wide, 80 feet long, and three stories high. There was a freight elevator at the northeast end of the building. There were tunnels under the sidewalk for storing coal.

The corner became the headquarters for the Swedish trade and the store a financial center for the Swedes. Immigrants, who spoke only Swedish, were able to buy steamship tickets from the store owners when they wanted to visit their native land. Oscar also sold money orders for foreign exchange when people sent money back home.

The double store on the main floor was occupied by the Anderson men with a full stock of dry goods, clothing, crockery, groceries, and novelties. On the third floor was the firm of Benson & Carlson who sold furniture. On the ground floor, with entrances along the Wilson Street hill, were A. I. Anderson's tailor shop, John Micholson's Meat Market, and Benson & Thoreson's boot and shoe store.

From time to time the Andersons altered their offerings. John went into the dry goods business, and Oscar took over the grocery business. A partition was built dividing the first floor. Later it was removed and the business again consolidated.

Eventually John and his sons Dave and Edgar went into the grocery business, and Oscar went into the dry goods business with a new partner August Sevetson. They divided the first floor again and it has been divided ever since.

Over the years a number of people occupied the second story. In the 1920s, Oscar Hubbard, M. D., and Dr. F. E. Downs, a dentist, had offices there. Nels Herman ran his real estate loan and insurance business from the second story. Elaine Cannon had her workshop/studio there for quite a few years where she made the miniatures for which she became famous. Later the space was converted to apartments.

Through these many interior changes, the exterior has changed very little. Shingles have been added on the lower levels. Originally there was a roof over the entrances on the ground floor going east down the hill.

In the '30s W. L. Anderson and his son Kenneth still occupied the south half of the first floor as a dry goods store. Axel Wallman was the ticket agent for the Aurora Elgin and Fox River Electric Company and sold tickets from his grocery store in the north half of the Block.

In the early 1940s, the south half was still Anderson Dry Goods. The north half was the Colonial Sweet Shop, owned by Harry Sutton. It also served as the Aurora-Elgin Bus Depot.

During World War II, William's daughters, Mary Anderson and Virginia Freedlund, kept open the dry goods business in case one of their brothers wanted to run it after he returned from the war. That didn't happen, and Mary took over the business in 1945 and continued it until 1972 when she retired.

The south half continued as a general dry goods store but eventually carried only ladies ready-to-wear. Joe Marconi purchased the Block when Mary retired and opened Ms. Donali which has since moved across the street. The north half of the Block has remained a restaurant.

Business was carried on in the building by the Anderson family for 90 years. Oscar ran it for 31 years; son William L. ran it for 31 years; and granddaughter Mary was in business for 28 years.

Oscar Anderson was responsible, too, for two of the lovely old homes along Wilson and Jackson Streets. He built one on the southeast corner. He lived there until son William married in 1885 and moved into it. Oscar then built a house directly west across Jackson Street for himself.[6]

Thompson and Shaw Grocery, 15 East Wilson Street

The stone and brick building at 15 East Wilson Street was built in 1906 by James A. Thompson and Herman W. Shaw for use as a grocery store. Today it is owned by John A. Budilovsky and houses his law and real estate offices along with other businesses.

An agreement dated March 28, 1906, between Thompson and Shaw and Albert Snow, the owner of the building adjoining on the west read in part, "Thompson and Shaw are about to erect on their premises and along the division line between the tracts, a stone and brick building, the west wall of which is to be built of stone and of the following dimensions: the basement 22 inches thick; the first story 18 inches thick; the second story 16 inches thick. Said building is to be 90 feet in length, extending from the north line of Wilson Street."[7]

The land has held several buildings and housed numerous businesses. Evidence of wooden structures on the site before 1906 is found in several sources. An 1860 map shows a long narrow building and an 1869 map shows what appears to be a smaller building set back about 20 feet from Wilson Street used as a blacksmith shop.

An 1885 fire insurance map shows a long narrow wooden building, the front two-thirds, which is two-story, used for groceries and the back single story one-third as a restaurant. A second story was added above the restaurant at some time. Restorers found evidence of a wooden wall inside the masonry suggesting that Thompson and Shaw placed a brick wall over a wooden one on the east.

James Thompson and his partner Willis Grimes had run a grocery store on this corner before the building was erected. As might be guessed, Thompson and Grimes were brothers-in-law. In 1891 Herman Shaw bought Grimes' half interest. He was a brother-in-law as well. Mrs. Grimes and Mrs. Thompson were Shaw's sisters.

The first discernible records of the land is a sale from Lester Barker and Alanson House to Nathan Lord in 1845. In 1865 Lord sold the land to Orasmus Wilson, Isaac's brother, who the following year sold it to the Donovan family who lived in Elgin in 1860. John and Richard Donovan had a blacksmith shop on the spot in 1867. In 1895 Miss Ann Donovan sold the land to Thomas Snow who in 1896 sold it to Thompson and Shaw. The men had apparently rented the building prior to that time. After Thompson's death, Shaw continued in business at the location until 1931.

Until 1966 or '67, the building remained a grocery store, first an A & P; then a National Tea; and from the early '50s, it was the Community Cash Market owned by John and Peter Gricunas.

Other occupants have been V. E. Anderson Realty Company in the 1970s and several chiropractors from 1978-83. The building is listed as vacant in the city directories beginning in 1983 except for Woyton Sales, Inc., in 1987. However, the trust department of the Gary-Wheaton Bank and the Kane County Insurance Company used the building in recent years. Because there were offices on the second story, there were undoubtedly other occupants who were not listed in city directories.

Michael Hoge of the Pride of the Fox Masonry Company restored the exterior. He pointed out the three colors of stone and mortar on the facade. There is black glazed brick held together by a mortar into which a black die was injected. "This was typical of the early 1900s," Hoge said. The rough cut brick at the top was probably placed there in the 1940s. Hoge suggests that the original parapet may have given way and was replaced. Red brick and stone trim add interest to the color and design of the building's front. Blond brick was added to the foundation during the recent restoration.

Much of the interior of the building has been redone. When Budilovsky acquired the building, the main floor was one large area though it had earlier been divided. He again divided the space, this time into six offices. A hall running along the east wall provides access to the offices.

The original windows were lengthened to allow more light into the hallway. The nine-inch wide sills and window wells have been lined with mirrors to provide reflected light. An interesting effect is achieved when this modern touch is combined with the old.

As much of the original materials was saved as could be. Glass from the second-story windows is used in the first-story ones. On the second story, the original two-inch wide, white pine flooring and the old woodwork remain. Office doors are wood with the old frosted glass windows, looking much as they probably did in the early 1900s. The basement has been converted to storage areas, offices, and a conference room.

A bricked-up doorway in the middle of the exterior east wall was found. It went to a stairwell that once ran through the middle of the building. New brick was reset so that the cut lines of the old door no longer show. An entrance and stairwell are at the north end of the building.[8]

240 East State Street

Entering the north door of the old Louise White School, one is struck by the beauty of the interior brick walls and the hardwood floors constructed in 1893-94 after fire destroyed the original school.

It was on Tuesday, January 10, 1893, that the first stone school house of District #6 East Batavia was consumed by fire. That building had been erected in 1860.

156

It is the "new" building that is the home of Pedals, Pumpers, and Rolls. This building was dedicated on New Year's Day, 1894. It stood upon a beautiful strip, surrounded by stately shade trees on the romantic banks of the Fox River. A belfry was located on the north side.

Built of Batavia limestone, it contained two stories with nine rooms. It had three convenient exits and two large stairways. The stone walls were 20-22 inches thick.

There was radiator heat that could warm the entire building with only five pounds of steam.

This magnificent structure closed as a school in 1978. Roger and Carol Dayton purchased the run-down building, filled with nothing but trash, in 1985. Several businesses had used it in the interim. In 1980 the old school was placed on the national Register of Historic Places.

The first thing the Daytons did was to build luxurious living quarters on the second floor and begin moving their business into the 1927 brick addition. In the gymnasium they added a floor at ground level, cutting its height in half because the floor of the original gym is below ground. This provided storage space for their collection and for customers' pieces on which they are working.

The final phase of their move was in 1992 when their store occupied the north classrooms and the adjoining hallways on the first floor. One of the old classrooms is the office and music roll room.[9]

12 East Wilson Street

The one thing that had been constant in the eighty-four years that Gary-Wheaton Bank of Batavia had served the community was that it had remained in its original home; but that, too, changed.

Batavia National Bank had a capitalization of $50,000 in 1909. Dr. Augustine purchased the bank's first stock and was its first president. Alexander Mitzell was its first vice-president and

Nicholas Johnson, its first cashier. It became Batavia Bank until it was purchased by Gary-Wheaton Bank. Soon, the Gary-Wheaton Banks were purchased by the First Chicago Holding Company.

Since its founding in 1909, Batavia National Bank, has undergone changes in ownership, changes in name, and changes in the services it provides, but it had always remained at home at 12 East Wilson Street in a building it purchased from Dr. John C. Augustine in 1920. At the time the dry goods store of Julia Kline & Co., the tailor shop of E. L. Latcham and Alex Wainright, the Kraft Garment Factory, the Odd Fellows Hall, and other offices were also in the building.

No doubt Wilson Street was "the place" to be in 1909. Many businesses were located between River Street and the river, and many of Batavia's factories were located just to the north. Today Randall Road is the place to be and the bank is on North Randall Road. The last day of business for the bank in its original facility was January 15, 1993.[10]

----

[1] Land description records at the Kane County Recorder's Office in Geneva.

[2] The Batavia Manufacturing Company was located near Shumway's Foundry. They manufactured the Nichols' Centennial Wind Mill, a tire shrinker, and several other related farm items.

[3] **Batavia Herald,** April 28, 1893.

[4] Originally published July 24, 1991.

[5] Originally published July 24, 1991.

[6] Thanks to Mary Anderson and Virginia Freedlund for their great help with the history of the Anderson Block.

[7] Land records in the Kane County Recorder's Office in Geneva.

[8] Originally published August 19, 1992.

[9] Originally published September 16, 1992.

[10] Originally published January 15, 1993.

Tower Business Center

Photo Courtesy of Batavia Historical Society

van Nortwick Paper Company

Batavia National Bank

Thompson & Shaw Groceries

Photos courtesy Batavia Historical Society

East Side School built in 1893

Photo courtesy of Batavia Historical Society

Anderson Brothers Block

PUBLIC PLACES

Depot Museum, 155 Houston Street

The Depot Museum, home of the Batavia Histori-
cal Society, started as a passenger depot for the
Chicago and Aurora Branch Railroad. In 1855 the
railroad became the Chicago, Burlington and
Quincy Railroad and eventually, the Burlington-
Northern.

Originally the plan in 1849 was to build only
the twelve miles of track from Aurora to Turner
Junction[1] through Batavia and to call the new railroad the Aurora Branch.

A meeting was held late in 1848 to consider
building a railroad to the north. John vanNortwick,
chief engineer of the Galena Road, and possibly
the moving spirit behind the Aurora Branch, was
at the meeting.

By February, as a director, vanNortwick repre-
sented those who wished to link Aurora with the
Galena and Chicago Rail Road which would reach
Turner Junction in the spring of 1849. Later he
served as the fifth president of the railroad from
1857-65.

On September 2, 1850, after the track was laid
from Turner Junction to Batavia, the first passenger train left Batavia at 6:30 a.m. to make connec-
tions with the Galena. This train was made up of
an engine named the "Pioneer" and a single coach
borrowed from the Galena.

On October 22, 1849, a passenger depot was
authorized for Batavia at Webster and VanBuren
Streets. When the present depot was built in 1855,
the original one was moved to its present location
about one block north, and it became the freight
depot."[2]

The new depot became the Depot Museum. It is
a broad-eaved "shed" depot in a board and batten
frame in Gothic Revival style. There have been a

162

few exterior repairs, but the building is basically unchanged.

During most of the life of the building as a depot, a passenger agent lived in the two back rooms downstairs and in the second story, while the offices were in the front room and storage was in the lower level.

It can't be determined that an agent always lived in the depot, but as early as 1857, a city directory shows that Agent Edward Dixon lived there. In 1867 Agent Thomas Cleveland's residence is given as the C. B. & Q. Depot. Cleveland was the agent from 1860-81. In 1911 Edward and Sarah Harris lived there, and Edward was the C. B. & Q. agent.

By 1924 Ralph and LuLu Richards lived in the depot, and Ralph is the agent. By 1932 W. Norman and Bessie Edwards reside there, and Edwards is listed as an employee of the C. B. & Q. Florian Walter is the freight agent but lives on Elizabeth Street. By 1943 the Walter family had moved to the Depot. Passenger service must have stopped by this time because Walter is listed as the freight agent who lives in the passenger depot. Walter was an agent for seventeen years.

The Walters purchased the depot from the railroad about 1945 because they wanted to improve the heating system by replacing the pot belly stove with an oil furnace and duct work to heat the upstairs. Until then only a hole in the floor of the second story had allowed heat to the upstairs.

After Walter's death, Bob Adams became the agent and purchased the depot from the Walter family. Adams resigned in 1964, and Charles Hodson became the agent until the depot closed in 1966.

Mr. and Mrs. Adams continued to live in the building until it was sold to Art Swanson, Phil Carlson, and Phil Elfstrom in 1971. A citizens' committee raised the money necessary to move the depot to 155 Houston Street on October 12, 1973, and to restore it for use as a museum by the Batavia Historical Society in cooperation with the Batavia Park District which maintains it.[3]

City Hall, Shumway Avenue

Researching the old city hall raised as many questions as it gave answers. Exactly when the building was built remains a mystery.

The date carved on the outside of the building is nearly illegible. It appears to read 1880 something. Some persons believe it's '89, some '87, some '93 and others '95.

An 1892 map shows that the city hall and electric plant is at the corner of First Street and what is now Shumway Avenue. It's difficult to tell from the map, whether the building is the same shape as it is today. It's certain that the land on which the building sits once belonged to John vanNortwick.

Perhaps the real answer to when the magnificent building of Batavia limestone was built is that it was somewhere around 1888 and that it was built in stages. The one-story south portion was Batavia's first municipal electric plant. To the east was a large detached shed to house the coal needed to make energy. Batavia had electricity in 1889. Therefore, that part of the building would have to have been built prior to that year.

Batavia voted to have a city form of government in 1891. It took effect on June 9 that year. City Council minutes neither before nor after that date indicate where the governing bodies met except "in the Council Chambers."

There is little question that the third section of the building on the north that is demolished was put into service in 1917 as a fire station. It had room for two trucks. A back room housed the old steam roller used by the city. Over the apparatus floor were rooms for the first paid fireman hired by the city. W. C. Thrun and his family lived in these quarters until July 1947 for Thrun worked around the clock every day.

Additions to the fire station portion were made in 1947 and 1959 as space was needed for more equipment.

Just as the building and its uses developed in stages, so did its abandonment. The city offices left the building in 1973 and moved into the portion of the Appleton Factory that stood west of the current government center. In 1983 the city offices moved to their current home, and the Police Department left the old city hall and took over the Appleton building the city vacated. The last of the fire department left the old station in 1988 after the opening of a fire house on West Main Street.

The city's first police department was housed in the old City Hall as was the city jail. The city hall portion held the clerk's office where citizens paid their utility bills. The council met for many years on the first floor.

The American Legion used the second floor until the council moved upstairs. The building was a center for youth activities and community events. Annual dinners were held on the second floor for Armistice Day celebrations. Mrs. Huldah Scheidler supervised the Huddle, a teenage recreation club, in the upstairs rooms for several years.

Unfortunately there's no complete written history of all the activities that were held during the building's nearly century of service to the city.[4]

240 East State Street/355 First Street

In the beginning there were two school districts in Batavia, #6, the east side, and #5, the west side. Grades 1-8 began as early as 1835 or '36, but the high schools came much later.

In 1879 the East Side High School graduated its first class. Prof. O. T. Snow was the superintendent for four years until he became superintendent of the West Side Schools.

The East Batavia Schoolhouse on Washington Avenue and State Street had three stories with two rooms on each floor. The high school occupied the top floor.

Only three years of work were required for graduation. The course of study included algebra, civics, general history, physical geography, botany, grammar, ancient history, philosophy, German, and drawing.

About five years later, Latin was introduced and courses in English and geometry were added. Chemistry, physics, and zoology were attempted, but there was no suitable equipment or space for experiments.

The trees around the school ground were planted by students; and additional land was purchased to enlarge the grounds. A small library with some reference books was collected.

In 1893 fire destroyed the building and practically all of its equipment. Classes moved to 4 East Wilson Street while a new building was being built on the old site.

In 1899 a commercial course was introduced, consisting of arithmetic, geography, law, and bookkeeping. With these additional courses, the school became a four-year one and was now accredited at the University of Illinois and Northwestern. The staff grew to a principal and two teachers, and a new assembly hall was built.

A high school was established on the west side in 1885 with classes at Central School on First Street. Old Main, as the school was first called, was considered quite spacious. There were two rooms on each of two floors and a hall with a stage on a third floor.

The high school occupied the south room on the second floor. O. T. Snow, the superintendent, also served as principal. The next year, the third-floor hall was divided into an assembly room and a classroom. Mrs. Mohr was the principal.

There were 2 years of Latin, 1 of algebra, 1 of plane geometry, and 1 of ancient and medieval history combined. English history was taught and although physiology, geology, botany, zoology, astronomy, and physics were offered, practically no lab work could be done for lack of equipment. German was extensive, and there were 4 years of English. The library consisted of a few reference works in a bookcase.

As enrollment increased in the elementary grades, the district purchased the old Methodist Church next door at 355 First Street. The high school occupied the second floor with a cloak room, an assembly hall, a classroom, and a well-equipped science lab.

Over the years, there were so many changes in superintendents and principals that the school fell backward. One superintendent attempted to reduce the 4-year course of study to 3 years. His plan broke up of an entire class so that only 1 or 2 students received diplomas.

Most of the science equipment was destroyed by students. Often while assigned to experiments, boys would instead hail the bakery wagon as it passed and by means of ropes enjoyed pie, cake, or rolls.

T. C. Fyre was hired. He tightened up the study and added music. Juniors and seniors held classes before and after the regular hours to make up missed work. They used Fyre's personal library, and this was the start of a real school library.

After Frye left, the high school began to run down again. In three years, the board concluded that more money had to be spent to raise the standard of the school. C. E. Mann became the new superintendent.

The high school faculty now consisted of the principal and one teacher. Later another teacher was added. The course of study was broadened, and the library was enlarged. Commercial subjects were dropped. Math offerings increased, and now there were four years of Latin and English. Interest in baseball and basketball began.

Frye was the first to suggest that the two districts consolidate. It was not until 1909 that the first definite step toward consolidation took place when Horace Bone was chosen as superintendent for both sides of the river.

Although the classes met separately, they united in athletics and considered themselves as one school. Work was made to correspond as far as possible in the two schools.

In 1910 the laboratories of the schools were united and a fairly well-equipped science lab was established on the first floor of the church/school building. The increased number of teachers permitted them to teach only the subject for which they were most suited.

Students attended the west side for some classes and the east side for others. The course of study widened, and much more effective work was achieved. Athletic participation grew. All this led to the final union of the district in the spring of 1911.

There were 30 graduates in the class of 1912. By the fall of 1912, the high school enrollment had increased to 180 with a prospect for continued growth. All of the second floor of the Church School was given over to the high school and a referendum was passed for a consolidated school on South Batavia Avenue on the former vanNortwick property. In 1966 this building became a junior high school which closed in 1993 when the Batavia Middle School on Raddant Road opened. It is slated for demolition to make room for a senior housing project.

As of 1995 in the eighty-five years since the schools consolidated, there have been but eight superintendents. In order of their service they are Dr. Horace Bone, Dr. H. C. Storm, J. B. Nelson, Arthur

Perry, William Dickson, Dr. James Clark, Dr. Stephanie Marshall, and Dr. Edward Cave.[5]

106 West Wilson Street

A new post office for Batavia opened on Randall Road in November 1993. The building of Indiana limestone and yellow brick on Wilson Street was retired after 65 years as the city's mail center. It was built at a cost of $77,353 and began service in July 1928. The funds for a new post office had been appropriated by Congress in 1913; but when war broke out in Europe, building costs rose beyond the appropriation.

In 1923 the Batavia Kiwanis Club took up the cause for the needed building, and finally Batavia had a federally funded post office building.

The first post office in Batavia was opened February 6, 1841, with Judge Isaac Wilson as its first postmaster. It was in the law office of Joseph Churchill, Wilson's son-in-law. For eight years, settlers had been going to Naperville for their mail.

Where Churchill's office was or when the post office moved from it is not known. In 1853 when Amos Moore was postmaster, it was in a corner of the Moore and Buck General Store at the southwest corner of Batavia Avenue and First Street.

When Edward Smith succeeded Moore (1861), he moved the post office into a building on Batavia Avenue just south of Wilson Street. There was a small steam running along this area, and the post office was in a building on the south side of the stream.

If newspaper accounts are correct, Smith later moved (date unknown) the post office into a small building on the south side of Wilson Street at the east edge of the pond.

In 1887, Willis Grimes, in his first appointment as postmaster, moved it two doors east into a building occupied by a bakery. This was on the site of the recently vacated post office on Wilson Street.

Still later, Grimes moved it into the vanNortwick Block across Shumway Avenue. It must have been in the east end of the building for the vanNortwick bank was in the west half. Here it remained until 1928.

City delivery was established in 1899, and rural free delivery in 1905. Parcel post service began in 1913. The first three city mail carriers were Charles Pierce, Charles Grimes, and C. J. Evans. They received a wage of $600 per year. The men had to make a house-to-house canvass to record the occupant and the names of all family members before they could begin delivery.

They walked the city until the government requested that they equip themselves with a horse. The mail was carried in a two-wheel box over an axle. The carrier rode on a step behind the horse and delivered on both sides as the animal progressed down the street. Later as the city grew and Walnut Street was added, the carriers went back to walking. Some routes are still walked though some are motorized with the carrier putting mail in curb side boxes without leaving the vehicle just as the first men on horses did.

Batavia has had 22 men and one woman serving as postmaster since 1841. The builders of the 1928 building added a lady's washroom sensing that there might some day be female employees working there. Little could they have imagined that 60 years later Julie Sabor would be in charge of postal service in their village.

Postmasters, including acting ones, and the year of their appointments are:

Isaac Wilson, 1841; John Waldron, 1846; Cornwall Brown, 1849; Amos Moore, 1853; Marvin Houck, July 1855; Amos Moore, September 1855; Edward M. Smith, 1861; Willis L. Grimes, 1886; James McMasters, 1890; Willis L. Grimes, 1893; Andrew Challman, 1897; Charles Briggs, 1900; Frank Hooker, 1911; John Geiss, 1913; Lloyd Wood,

1923; William Davis, April 1926; Carl Eckman, October 1926; Jacob Feldman, 1935; Leon Comstock, 1951; Paul Hendrickson, January 1953; August J. Meir, December 1953; Richard Markuson, 1959; Leon Comstock, 1961; Philip Talbot, 1962; Wayne T. Duerkes, 1985; Julie Sabor, 1988.[6]

---

[1] Now West Chicago.

[2] BATAVIA HISTORICAL SOCIETY NEWSLETTER (December 7, 1969.) An 1892 map confirms this as a freight depot.

[3] Originally published September 11, 1991.

[4] Originally published May 19, 1994.

[5] Originally published in three installments, October 20, November 3, November 10, 1993.

[6] Originally published November 3, 1993.

Photo courtesy Batavia Historical Society

west side school--elementary and high school
Old Main   Central School

West Side High School

Depot Museum

Downtown Post Office

Photo courtesy of Batavia Historical Society

Downtown consolidated high school

Note vanNortwick house to the right. The urns on the
pillars are now at Depot Museum. Note street lamps and no
traffic lights.

Photo courtesy of Batavia Historical Society

East Side Elementary and High School

Note children in windows and bell tower.

PLACES IN MEMORY

Batavia Institute, Jefferson Street at Union Avenue

Although the building that housed the Batavia Institute is still standing, the school has been gone for nearly 150 years. Because it was the first school serving high school youth in Batavia, it's worth remembering.

The impressive building at the west end of Union Avenue, which has become a symbol of Batavia's history, was built as a private town and boarding high school in 1854 at a cost of $15,000. Elijah Town, Denison Town, John vanNortwick, Joel McKee, and Rev. Stephen Peet[1] financed its building.

> These early immigrants, recognized the value of a "thorough and practical course of instruction composed of all studies necessary to prepare students for any college or to fit them for the active duties of life," quotes an early account of the institute.[2]

The building was described in an 1865 pamphlet.[3]

> The Institute Building is of cut stone, finished throughout, rooms high and airy, the upper story divided into society room; girls' study and sleeping hall, 60 x 30 feet; boys' hall and sleeping room, 50 x 60 feet; hall and stairway, with entrance to the belfry. The middle story contains the main school room, 70 x 40 feet, two large recitation rooms, hall, stairway, etc. The first floor above ground on the right is divided into a reception room, parlor, sitting-room and bed rooms, with kitchen, dining-room, and cellar below. On the left of the entrance hall is a similar division."

Two of the school's teachers, Prof. A. A. Griffith & family and Prof. S. N. Griffith and his family resided in this area.

The school did not exist very long because the year after it opened, Illinois passed the free public education law that ruled each community had to furnish its own public high school. Then Batavia's east side students went to high school in the old Louise White School on Washington Avenue, and the old church at 355 First Street became the West Side High School.

One year later, Batavia was one of several cities interested in securing the new normal school which was to be built in Illinois. It offered Batavia Institute with its ready-made plant and ample grounds plus $15,000 in cash to become the site of the new school. This was a large enough enticement to allow the selection committee to make Batavia one of three finalists for the school. Bloomington heard of Batavia's offer and upped theirs with additional land and cash. The new school was established at the new town of Normal.

Although there is evidence the institute was still operating in 1859, it apparently fell on hard times, for an attempt was made after the Civil War to reestablish it.

Another school pamphlet[4] states that in 1864, Judge Samuel Lockwood sold the grounds and buildings to A. A. Griffith. It doesn't appear that Lockwood owned it, but he was on the Board of Directors so perhaps that is why he is listed as the seller.

The property was sold for a small sum as an incentive to Griffith to build up the institute as a first-class preparatory school. As a further inducement, the citizens of Batavia guaranteed about $7,000 in tuition payable in four years by subscribing for a certain number of yearly scholarships at $125 each. This placed the school on a comparatively successful financial basis for its reopening.

A Literary Society was formed at the institute which was the beginning of a library. Books the students collected grew to a collection that was housed at various places over the years and eventually became the public library.

The school had a religious emphasis. There was a Theological Society to assist its students in gaining

175

knowledge of the Bible and Christian literature. The headmaster's aim was to conduct the institute upon the principles of "outspoken Christianity." Regular sessions were opened and closed with a reading from the Bible, singing and a prayer. Parents said which village church they wanted their children to attend, and the principal saw to it that their wishes were enforced.

The year after the Civil War when the school re-opened, there were 68 ladies and 58 gentlemen students. The tuition was $10 for a term of 11 weeks and there were 3 terms a year. Separate charges were made for supplies for each course of study such as $4.00 for a water-color class. There was an additional charge of $2.50-$4.50 per week for board. Students had to provide their own towels, napkins, and a pair of sheets and pillowcases.

Students were assigned living space under the special management of a teacher who directed their conduct in and out of school. The students occupied two large rooms with their teachers, who assisted them in acquiring habits of cleanliness and punctuality.

During their first year, students were offered such courses as algebra, astronomy, chemistry, Latin, French, composition, and elocution. The second year they studied geology, botany, mental science, moral science, Greek, composition, oration, and geometry. The last year geometry, history, logic, Constitution of the United States and Illinois, evidence of Christianity, trigonometry, and special instruction in elocution were offered.

Students couldn't engage in any association between men and ladies, games of chance, intoxicating drinks, profane or obscene language, visitation on the Sabbath or during study hours, clamorous noise in and around the institution, throwing things from the windows, use of gun powder on the premises without permission, and absence from the room after evening signal for study hours.[5] It was suggested that students unwilling to obey these rules should not apply for admission.

Prof. Griffith apparently couldn't save the school for in 1867 Dr. Richard J. Patterson, John Patterson, and Seymour Wolcott bought the building and established a mental hospital for ladies. Patterson furnished the old school rooms with beautifully carved beds, huge ornate chests, and other appropriate furniture and changed its name to Bellevue Place.

Wagner School, 34W144 Giese Road

Another building still stands, but the school it contained is gone. The memories of Wagner School remain in many minds. It is now a remodeled home in a modern subdivision just west of Kirk Road.

Joel McKee owned the land on which Wagner School sat for over seventy years. He sold portions of it to various farmers, and by 1862 Charles Schimelpfenig owned much of it. In August 1880 Charles sold half an acre to the trustees of School District No. 9 for $50. The land lay just east of a pond. In 1952 the land was deeded back to Irvin Schimelpfenig, a grandson of Charles'. Irvin and his wife Mary converted the school into a home and rented it until Joyce Cregier and her daughter Jodie of St. Charles purchased it for renovation.

The county built Wagner School, but the exact date it opened is unknown. It can be assumed that it might have been in the fall of 1880 as it would not have taken long to raise the one-room building. It closed in 1943 when there were only four boys attending, and one of those was moving away. Batavia School District #101 absorbed the area, and the boys went "into town" to school. The building was used for a while afterward for such activities as passing out ration coupons during World War II to those living in the old school district.

Although the Creigers gutted the interior and lowered the ceilings, the exterior has not been changed. The house has a living room, bathroom, kitchen, two bedrooms, and a laundry room.

Irene Arbizzani, Joyce's mother, graduated in 1927 from Wagner and remembers the white school house with a merry-go-round in the yard. "The south entrance with the porch is the same as when I went to school there," she said. She also remembers going to the courthouse in Geneva to take eighth-grade exams to get into high school.

Three ladies who taught in the school fondly recall their time there. Mrs. Hattie Seagrist of Aurora taught there in 1918-19. It was her first teaching job, and she was just out of Batavia High School. H. C. Storm called her senior class together and asked how many wanted to be teachers. Six girls indicated they planned to take the teacher's examination. Storm held a special class for them during the year for he said they would never pass the eighteen-hour exam without help. "He taught us what we needed to know," Seagrist said.

Seagrist recalls six students in 1918, including a boy in the first grade, a girl in the third grade, two boys in the fifth, and a boy and a girl in the eighth grade. "Her goal," she said, "was to teach the first graders to read, write, and do numbers, and to get the eighth graders to pass the county examination for high school."

Mrs. Dorothy Bechtold of North Aurora taught twenty students at Wagner School from 1928-30. She recalls a pump organ in one corner which one of the eighth grade girls played when the students sang. The building was heated by a potbelly stove which was lighted each morning by Bechtold using corn cobs and kerosene. "This was a dangerous chore," she said. Light came from the many windows on each side of the building. If an activity were held at night, there were kerosene lights with reflectors behind them. When these were used, Bechtold and her students had to clean them the next day. Some of the lamps are still in the attic.

The teachers and Arbizzani recall the girls' and boys' backyard toilets—still in use when the school closed. The two cloak rooms were segregated, too, just inside the porch door. They remember a full-hour for lunch, everyone eating their homemade lunches together, and the children ice skating on the pond during the winter. "The children played such games as pom pom pull-a-way; andy, andy, over; and baseball during lunch," recalls Bechtold.

The teachers cleaned the school with a mop and broom and cold water from the front-yard pump. The big boys helped bring the water in for the hand washing basin in one of the cloak rooms.

Mrs. Shirley Walsh of Batavia was the teacher in 1943 when the school closed. When she began two years earlier, there was electricity and a furnace. The back room, now the laundry room, was used to store coal and kindling for the heater.

Seagrist remembers the boys filling a wooden pail from the front yard pump and everyone drinking from the same dipper. When Walsh was there, the pump filled a crock with a faucet. The organ had been replaced by a piano, but the children still skated on the pond.

Because the school was "out in the country," the teachers had to find transportation to it. Seagrist rode the "third rail" for five minutes, got off at

Wagner Road and walked the two blocks up the hill to the school on Giese Road.

Bechtold stayed one year in the area with the Milhorn family, but the second year she rode a bus from North Aurora, up Route 25 to downtown Batavia, then the "third rail" to Wagner Road. Walsh drove the two and one-half miles from her home on the east side and was able to park her car in a garage there. In bad weather, however, she rode the "third rail."[6]

Octagonal House, 264 Forest Avenue

"We continue to build in the same square form. Cannot some radical change for the better be adopted for both the external and interior form of houses? Why not take a pattern from nature? Her forms are mostly spherical," wrote Orson Fowler.[7] To support his view, he drew plans for eight-sided houses. Not many were built, but one was in Batavia.

Fowler was not an architect, but a New York City phrenologist. Phrenology was a popular pseudo-science which said character could be read by the shape of one's head. The house on Forest Avenue could be fancied a head, wearing a pointed hat. The chimney ran through the middle of the house and topped the eight-sided, peaked roof. "This gave an appearance of a 'witch's hat'," said Shirley Vest Walsh, a long time owner of the house. "I never had many trick or treaters," she said, laughing. "Children were afraid of the witch's house."

Isaac Wilson first owned the land on Forest Avenue. By 1855 it belonged to I.S.P. Lord who sold a large piece of it to John McEwen for $367.30 in 1864. Descendants of McEwen say that he built the octagon house, and records seem to substantiate that. Why he chose the unusual shape is not known.

McEwen owned the house until 1900 when he sold it to William Duckett who kept it only one year before selling it to Frederick Nurnberg, who worked for the Appleton Company. Nurnberg died, and it was sold in 1906 to John Blacksmith, a thresher, who in 1914, sold it to George Blacksmith, who worked for the U. S. W. E. & Pump Co.

John had wanted to sell it to William Davis, Walsh's father, but her mother refused to live so far out in the country. The city limits were still at the east end of the property in 1956 when Walsh and her husband Arthur Vest bought it.

George Blacksmith sold the house to John T. E. Johnson in 1919. Years later it was unwittingly rented to bootleggers who called themselves George and Mabel Davis. The renters emptied their mash into Mahoney's Creek. Lyle Reinsdorff was a cattle dealer whose animals grazed downstream from the octagonal house. They became very contented cows, but staggered when they walked.[8] In 1938 the original barn on the property burned when the Davis' still blew up.

By 1944 the home belonged to Robert and Virginia Bricket. Virginia sold it in 1952 to Morris Barron who operated a garment factory in Batavia. He sold the house to the Vests.

The eight sides of the house formed nearly a circle. Builders have told Shirley that this made it nearly tornado proof. Each of the eight sides was eleven feet long. On the first floor, the rectangle formed by opposite angles included the original living room, small kitchen, a bedroom and dining room. The spaces left over formed closets and the triangular front entrance hall. There were no doors on many of the interior openings. A rectangular addition to the east included a kitchen and a bathroom. The bath tub had to be brought in through an opening cut in the outside wall because of the narrow exterior doorways.

The interior staircase was so narrow that furniture had to be taken to the one-half upper story through the upstairs windows. The second floor was divided into two large bedrooms.

Arranging furniture was fairly easy despite an angle every eleven feet. Three sides formed the front wall, placing many windows in the living room. It was like being in a big bay window.

The exterior was sided with gray asphalt shingles that resembled rock. Underneath were medium-width, white clapboards. There was a shallow cellar under the entire house. A backyard well still furnished the only water in 1990.

There were many beautiful spruce and maple trees in the large yards, and Mahoney Creek runs through the north yard. The front windows looked across the street at a woods.[9]

The house has been razed to make way for several new homes.

Revere House, 131 South Batavia Avenue

Charles Ballard bought land for a hotel from Barker and House in 1840 near the vanNortwick homes on Batavia Avenue and not too far from the farm of James Rockwell.

Charles was the husband of Fanny vanNortwick, a daughter of William's, making him a brother-in-law to Rockwell. The Ballards came to Big Woods as soon as William sent for his family. Charles was involved with the eastern conglomerate; but soon was out of favor with his brother-in-law, John, and went out on his own.

It is reported that Charles built his hotel/tavern in 1837, though he did not own the land until 1840. Ballard's hotel was replaced by a three-story native limestone structure built by John Clark. The building had porches facing east across the front of all three stories.

Just when the hotel became The Revere House isn't known, but it can be guessed. In 1857 an advertisement under the heading *Revere House* states that H. S. Moore and B. F. Davis recently leased the well-known house formerly called the *Worsley Hotel* and were now **"prepared to accommodate boarders and travelers visiting Batavia."** The house had been newly furnished and improvements added for the comfort of guests. Passengers were to be carried to and from the depot free of charge.[10]

In 1880 William Howell was the hotel keeper, and he, his wife, daughter, and 19 boarders lived there. Included in these were William Blair, the hotel cook, the hotel baker, 2 hotel waiters, an ice merchant, 2 well diggers, a blacksmith, a jeweler, a stone mason, Dr. John C. Augustine, physician, Charles Osgood of Osgood and Shumway Foundry, and several laborers.[11]

The hotel changed hands often with Mr. and Mrs. Elworthy in charge for many years. In 1929 Mrs. Rowlands was managing the business which by then was known as the Batavia Hotel.

Revere House was the center of social and business life in Batavia. Many came to listen to the wit and humor of the period and fill up on roasted chicken at banquets. Young people came to dance to the music of a stringed orchestra, and business men conferred in the tavern lobby.

Drummers who came to call on local trade stayed over night, and locals gathered in the lobby to hear these knights of the road tell of folks over in DuPage or DeKalb Counties.

Influential people gathered during the late 1850s to discuss the crying issue of the day, abolition. They also discussed the tall Illinois rail-splitter who had been chosen to be the Republican Party's nominee for president.

Here, too, the village bid farewell to the boys who marched away in response to President Lincoln's call for volunteers. And later a banquet and ball were held to welcome them home.

Years later, when the men who served in the Spanish-American War returned, a grateful public gathered again to sing the praises of its heroes.

By the early 1930s, the voices were stilled, and the hotel was vacant and in need of repair. In December

1938 city officials announced that they would tear down Revere House, by then a rather unsightly building. The porches had been torn away, and the property had been fenced off for it had become a hazard to passers-by.[12]

Fox River Sanitarium, 831 North Batavia Avenue

Chicago Consumptive Aid Society

FOX RIVER SANITARIUM · · BATAVIA, ILL.

In 1926 when Bessie Hirschberg worked in a cigar factory in Chicago, she found facilities for caring for the tubercular poor were inadequate. A diagnosis of TB meant isolation for the patient, and there were few if any places for the poor. Hirschberg began collecting pennies from the poor and formed the Chicago Consumptive Aid Society. Bessie's husband saw an ad in the newspaper offering river-front land for sale in Batavia. When $150,000 was raised, the Society took possession of the land, and the Fox River Sanitarium was built in the early 1930s.

Batavia was chosen because it was far enough from Chicago to escape the city's noises, but close enough that patients could be near loved ones and be comforted by frequent visits. A Chicago and North Western commuter train ran along the river and visitors from Chicago could get to the hospital by train.

The Fox River Sanitarium was a pioneer in TB care. It was like a modern hospital with sunny rooms, wards, solaria, modern operating rooms, sterilizing equipment, X-ray facilities, and a dental facility so fine that it was said patients lost all fear of going to the dentist.

Most patients in the sanitarium were those who were in advanced stages of the disease. They were all from Chicago, mostly of the Jewish faith, and stayed for prolonged periods. Usually there were about 50 patients in the hospital at any one time.

In 1940 the hospital treated 128 patients. There were 82 men and 46 women ranging in ages from 15 to 60 years. In that year the Society raised and gave to the hospital $65,275 of which $50,000 was used to run the hospital and treat patients.

Nurses worked for 32 cents an hour, 10 hours a day, and did all types of work. A private duty nurse worked 20 hours a day and slept in the room with the patient.

The sanitarium was a town unto itself. There were out buildings around the hospital, and it had its own wells and sewage disposal plant. There were cement walks leading from one building to another, and the grounds were beautifully landscaped.

All food served in the hospital was prepared in adherence to Jewish culinary laws. Nearly all food not grown on the property was donated through the society in Chicago and brought to Batavia by train.

The hospital was built on land previously owned by Hamilton Browne. He was a railroad organizer and builder and operated coal mines in Iowa. Beginning in 1904 he engaged in railroad building in Illinois.

In 1900 Browne purchased the Calumet Stock Farm from David and Cornelia Brown of Geneva. This land was on Route 31 on both sides of Fabyan Parkway.

Hamilton and his wife, Mary Louise Napier, lived in a very large white house. Whether Browne built it or it was the residence of the stock farm is not known. The first patients at the sanitarium who were mobile stayed in the house. It stood in the clump of trees still near the Michealsen Center according to Jeff Schielke. The old curving, driveway to the house is visible just south of the intersection of Fabyan Parkway and Batavia Avenue.

Jeff remembers when the house was razed in 1974. He recalls it as a two- or three-story Victorian that was neglected and badly overgrown. The house and the sanitarium were both neglected after the hospital closed for people were afraid the buildings were contaminated with germs. Even when the hospital was in operation, local citizens pretty much ignored it, according to Jeff. "**It was out of town at the time, the patients were all from Chicago, and the locals just didn't pay much attention to it,**" he said.

The society soon built a long wooden building for bed patients, constructed with rooms on either side of a long hallway, all opening onto a porch so that patients could be outdoors in all weather. This was thought to be an aid in curing tuberculosis. The cornerstone for the permanent building was laid in 1926.

The hospital closed in 1958 or 59. The Holmstad purchased the land in the early 70's for its campus after 3 or 4 years of planning. Schielke visited the hospital in 74 after Holmstad took possession. He recalls that all the equipment and supplies were still in place. The beds were made, and white sheets covered the examining tables. "**It was as though everyone just left, locked the doors and never came back,**" he said.

Perhaps because of her work at the Fox River Sanitarium, Bessie Hirschberg developed tuberculosis and became a patient in the hospital she had been instrumental in building and maintaining. She died there in 1937.

The building today is the Colonial House of Holmstad. The interior was gutted and completely renovated.[13]

Calumet Stock Farm, North Batavia Avenue

The land that became known as the Calumet Stock Farm was owned in 1872 by Salem B. Town. He had acquired the land from his father D. K. Most of this land was north of Fabyan Parkway and included 224 acres in a strip running for nearly a mile west from Batavia Avenue. Later 20 acres were added to the south side of Fabyan and west of today's Frank Lloyd Wright house.

Salem died in 1878, and the next year Joseph Shumway, a bachelor from New York bought the land. In 1882 he sold it to Cornelia and David Brown of Geneva.

As early as 1872, there is evidence that the land was used for raising stock. There are a house, barns, and stock pens shown on a plat map. The Fox River Valley Rail Road ran through the property, making it easy to ship animals to market.

In January 1891 Cornelia Brown, by then a widow, sold the stock farm to Lorin Davies from Chicago. It is probable that he named it the Calumet Stock Farm, for this is the first time the name appears in land records. In June of that year, a newspaper article reads. **"Roy Wilkes, the great pacing stallion with a record of 2:08 1/4 owned by the Calumet Stock Farm at Batavia is featured on the cover of this week's issue of *Clark's Horse Review*."** Roy Wilkes was one of the fastest horses in the world at the time.[14]

The article also described the farm. **"Several months ago Mr. Davies, the owner of the farm came out from Chicago, bringing with him a big string of fast ones. The farm is a fine one. The fences are all tight and there is no barb wire. The house and barns are lighted with electric wires, and there is a telephone connection to the Chicago office. There are 60 good-sized stalls. A new 3/4 mile track has been built, and everything is conducted in a first-class manner.**[15] Owners of race horses from across America visited the farm.

In December 1898 the two-story home on the property burned down for lack of fire fighting facilities. The fire started when a stove pipe from the kitchen which ran through the attic became hot and set some cobwebs on fire.

Mr. Davies apparently over extended himself and was unable to meet the mortgage on the farm. It reverted to Mrs. Brown who by now had moved to Massachusetts.

It was then that Hamilton Browne and his wife, Mary Louise bought it in 1900, all 240 acres for $25,000. The property was eventually divided. Some was owned by the Chicago Consumptive Aid Society which sold the land north of Fabyan Parkway to the Campana Sales Company and some of it to the Kane County Forest Preserve.

Kane County Alms House, Fabyan Parkway
This home for the poor and mentally insane was located northeast of Batavia from June 1852 until it was phased out 117 years later at the end of 1969.

Before the Alms House was opened, the poor were placed with individuals in private homes. They were housed for a small fee, paid by the township. Each township had a commissioner of the poor who arranged these placements.

In the spring of 1852, the Board of Supervisors bought the 179-acre farm belonging to Elijah Lee for $61 per acre.

James Hotchkiss was appointed the home's first superintendent. By September that first year, there were seventeen people there.

Lee's buildings were used to house the residents until after the Civil War when money became available to build a three-story stone building at a cost of $18,000. W. P. Barker of Batavia did the stone work on this new building.

By 1893 there were 2 main buildings. The newer one was 4 stories high. An addition for the mentally insane was erected soon after. It was 20 x 24 feet, 2 stories high and held 3 cells.

There was a huge horse barn which could house 24 animals, 14 of which were needed at any one time for hauling coal and performing other farm work. The cow barn had room for 60 cows. These provided milk for the residents with enough left over to sell.

A water tower and a deep well supplied the entire campus with water for cooking, cleaning, and fire protection. The complex was heated by steam generated on the grounds. An electrical plant was installed to supply light. It produced so much that there was enough left over to light the courthouse and jail in Geneva.

One problem of maintaining the home was solved at the turn of the century when the county spent $1,500 for a wash house. Laundry had become a problem for the nearly 200 residents and required a vast amount of labor. A new Empire laundry machine was installed. As many as 91 sheets could be put into the copper washer at one time. The wringing was done by centrifugal force and left the clothes ready for line drying.

There were a number of superintendents who managed the home over the years. Some early ones were Simeon McKinley, J. D. Sperry, and Alonzo Cook. Clark Wood served for 16 years from 1871 until his death. Then Seymour Keyes was superintendent for 17 years. He died in 1905, and John Micholson took over with Mrs. Micholson serving as matron. After he resigned in 1913, Frank Averill became manager and served for 21 years. He was followed by Robert Powell. When he died in 1951, Mrs. Powell and their son James took over. In 1960 Mr. and Mrs. Paul Willing supervised the farm and home until its closing.[16]

In 1970 the limestone residence facility was razed. Stone remnants from the old building were used by the Batavia Park District as part of a river beautification project along the eastern shore of the river south of the Wilson Street bridge.

The land was divided into several parcels. The north end was leased to be used as a landfill. The entrance to the landfill is the original entrance to the Alms House. The land to the west was used by the county for its correctional facilities. Land on the south side of Fabyan Parkway was sold and used as an industrial park.[17]

Zion Evangelical Church, 29 North VanBuren Street

As immigrants arrived in America, they did not all speak English. They built churches where only their language was spoken. Later two services were held, one foreign, one English.

Zion Evangelical, the oldest of the German Protestant (Methodist) Churches in Batavia, was organized in 1857. Rev. Rothermund of Aurora came to preach in private homes. The congregation's first regular minister was Rev. Gottlieb Mueller who was appointed by the Illinois Conference.

In 1866 the congregation erected the frame church on the site at the corner of VanBuren and State Streets. A parsonage adjoining the church to the south was built in 1873. It has been razed.

The congregation eventually merged with the Faith Church of the Brethren which meets at 613 North Van Buren. Holy Cross took over the old Zion church and used it until it moved to its new home on Main Street in 1994.

Music Hall, Shumway Avenue

In 1880 Batavia needed an opera house and a place to hold public meetings. A stock company was organized, and a number of shares were sold for $100 each. The Music Hall was erected on Shumway Avenue just north of the City Hall on land owned by John vanNortwick.

It was a wooden structure with a stone basement and had good stage equipment. The contractor and builder was James McMaster, a popular Republican postmaster.

After the hall was completed, some of the best shows on the road came to Batavia. Local talent also performed there. Citizens felt well repaid for building Music Hall although no one got rich because they owned stock. After the turn of the century all shares were sold to the vanNortwicks.

Having the auditorium on the ground floor was one of the most popular features of the building. It was considered one of the most convenient public halls on the Fox River, for while citizens of other cities had to climb long flights of stairs to get into their Opera House, Batavians did not. The facility had a seating capacity of 575.

When it was first completed, it was used extensively as a roller skating rink.

Eventually the Music Hall closed as a public hall and it was used as a job printing office. About 1912 it was reopened as an opera house, and in 1914 Mrs. E. M. Eberman began showing motion pictures there.

In October 1917 Joe Burke and S. E. Shaffner of Chicago leased the building from the vanNortwicks for a movie theater. They called it the Vanity Theater and later the Capitol Theater. Soon Burke bought the building.

In 1948 Valos Brothers purchased the movie house and ran it for several years intermittently. Since then the old Opera House has been used by a number of small business establishments.[18]

Glenwood Park Transient Camp

Early in 1934 the state was given land once owned by the Chicago, Alton and Elgin Railroad because taxes on the property had risen so high it was no longer profitable for the railroad to maintain it. For two decades the park had been a popular summer picnic grounds operated and supervised by the railroad who ran special cars to the scene.

In July of 1934 the park was converted into a transient camp, and the federal government moved a group of men into it from a similar site at Algonquin. This was a part of President Franklin Roosevelt's New Deal program to help pull the country through the depression.

Twenty-four dormitories were built, a restaurant and recreation building was set up, stoves put in, washrooms were constructed, and modern plumbing and showers were installed.

The men who inhabited the camp were used on PWA and CWA projects in and around Batavia. The most notable work they accomplished was the reconditioning of Island Park.

By 1937 the last of the 480 men who'd been stationed at Glenwood Park were released in groups of ten or twelve at a time. By the end of June, there were but four men left in the "little village" just one mile south of Batavia. They left the government's store of wheel barrows, trucks, shovels, picks and other tools that the men had used on their projects.

City officials and the Batavia Police Department were happy to see the camp close though some tavern owners may have regretted it. The inhabitants had been a problem for the local administration for three years because of the intoxication and disorderly conduct of the men on city streets. The camp officials were warned repeatedly that women and children lived in this community and disliked the unruly group.[19]

---

[1] Peet, a Congregational minister, was in Batavia from 1852-54.

[2] From archives at the Depot Museum.

[3] From archives at the Depot Museum.

[4] From archives at the Depot Museum.

[5] One wonders under what conditions permission would have been granted to use gun powder.

[6] Originally published January 22, 1992.

[7] Professor Orson Squire Fowler, **A HOME FOR ALL; OR THE GRAVEL WALL, AND OCTAGON MODE OF BUILDING** (1850) Introduction.

[8] A recollection from Don Schielke.

[9] Originally published October 24, 1990.

[10] **Batavia Weekly Argus**, April 19, 1857.

[11] From the 1880 Kane County census for Batavia.

[12] Most of the information about Revere House came from newspaper articles in the **Batavia Herald**, November 29, 1929, and December 2, 1938.

[13] Thank you to Ruth Strand for her help with the Fox River Sanitarium.

[14] The **Aurora Daily Beacon**, June 13, 1891.

[15] The **Aurora Daily Beacon**, June 13, 1891.

[16] Much of this information came from articles that ran almost weekly in Kane County newspapers. Primary sources for this section were the **Aurora Beacon-News**, February 7, 1970, an article written by John Gustafson; **Batavia Herald**, articles written in 1893, and **Hampshire Register**, May 10, 1907.

[17] John A. Gustafson & Jeffery D. Schielke **HISTORIC BATAVIA** (Batavia Historical Society 1980) 150.

[18] **Batavia Herald**, March 11, 1920 and October 27, 1960.

[19] **Batavia Herald** June 21, 1972.

BATAVIA PLACES

Octagonal
House

Zion
Evangelical
Church

Photo courtesy Batavia Historical Society

Wagner
School

Kane County Alms House at Batavia

Photos courtesy Batavia Historical Society

Revere House

INDEX

a town house, the residence of the 1990s

In the 1990s, neighborhoods are identified by their sub-division names. This one is Georgetown I on Clybourne Street.

Will anyone a century from now be writing about its history?

Books by Marilyn Robinson

The Frerichs Tree 1795-1975

Compilation of 1860 DeKalb County, Illinois, Census

Gleanings from the Christian Advocate and Journal and
Zion's Herald
September 1827-1831
(Compiled with Dolores Haller)

Little Town in a Big Woods

Little Town in a Big Woods, Revised

Batavia Places and the People Who Called Them Home

ABOUT THE AUTHOR

Marilyn Robinson came to Batavia in 1965 to teach at the high school. Her first year was the last one the downtown campus was used as a high school.

She left teaching in 1988 and began researching and writing Batavia history. Her first book, **Little Town in a Big Woods,** was written for children in 1989. A revised edition of it was published in 1995. It is used extensively in the elementary schools of Batavia. The lower level exhibit at the Depot Museum is named for the book.

She began writing historic articles for the *Windmill Herald* shortly after the publication of **Little Town in a Big Woods.** She talks about Batavia history with third grade students in their schools and at the Depot Museum when they visit. She has had a twenty-five year interest in genealogical research.

Marilyn grew up and went to school in El Paso, Illinois. She holds degrees in education from Illinois State University and Northern Illinois University.